The Midnight Poet

The poet got up in the mid-of-the-night
And dug for a tablet in frenzy to write.
No notice he paid to his nightcap askew
Or how bold the wind through his cold attic blew.

Front cover art: "The Midnight Poet," by Janet L. Kragen

The Midnight Poet

Dwight R. Droz

Scandia Patch Press
Poulsbo, Washington

Copyright © 2003 by Dwight R. Droz

All rights reserved. No part of this book may be reproduced or transmitted in any form or by any means, electronic or mechanical, including photocopying, recording, or by any information retrieval system, without written permission of Scandia Patch Press.

Edited by:
    K. D. Kragen
    KaveDragen, Ink.
    http://kdkragen.com
    Bainbridge Island, Washington, USA

Product design/layout by K. D. Kragen
Cover design by Jerry George
Cover art by Janet L. Kragen & Dwight R. Droz
Image scanning/photo editing and restoration
    by Jerry George and K. D. Kragen
Technical Advisor, Don Taylor

Unless otherwise noted, all sketches and illustrations are by the author, who studied art with Mr. Nelson at Southern Branch University in Pocatello, Idaho.

Scandia Patch Press
633 Northwest Scandia Road
Poulsbo, Washington 98370
http://kdkragen.com/scandia

Printed in the U.S.A.
10 9 8 7 6 5 4 3 2 1

Dedicated to my beloved wife, Pauline

CONTENTS

Introduction: Dining at Mitzel's

The Kite Fliers

1. A Girl With Corn-Tassel Hair — 10
2. To A Friend — 18
3. The Forsaken Bough — 20
4. The Greatest Gift — 22
5. No Returning — 24
6. With Weary Heart — 26
7. In Twenty Years — 28
8. Then and Now — 30
9. Love Unrequited — 32
10. The Kite Fliers — 34
11. Mount Harrison — 36
12. The Periscope of Time — 38

Chitchat

13. Party Chitchat — 46
14. Nilean Capers — 50
15. The Haven (Grasshopper) — 52
16. Childhood Playmates — 54
17. Sunbonnet Babe — 56
18. Lamb Parade — 58

The Book of Zoz

19. Hamilton Hill — 64
20. Algernon of Paris — 70
21. The Foundling — 72
22. Sick-a-muddy — 78
23. An impertinent Serpent — 80
24. Mountain Bouncin' — 84
25. Herminfouth and the Purple Tiger — 94
26. Tales from Lamplight Lane — 108

Old Dogs and Nature

27.	The Beggar's Son	154
28.	The Coming Storm	156
29.	In the Clamor of a Shell	158
30.	Dead Fox Speaks	162
31.	Glittering Gold	164
32.	The Killing Floor	166
33.	The Rationeers	172
34.	Collywobble Requiem	176
35.	Lines To An Old Brown Dog	178
36.	The Poplars	180
37.	Hill Daisies	182
38.	Something September	184
39.	Earth and Heaven	186

The Midnight Poet

40.	The Midnight Poet	190
41.	A Teasdale Sea	192
42.	A Maiden Lies Dreaming	194
43.	The Skeletons	196
44.	Two Blind Men	198
45.	Fancy's Burial	202
46.	A Lament	204
47.	Sammy the Crow	206
48.	An Ode for the Road	212
49.	A Picassoan Lament	214
50.	Arathens and Antinens	218
51.	Little Paths	220
52.	Only of Wood	222

The Midnight Poet

Introduction

Some cast aspersions on the poet who labors at every line. The poet is like the naturalist who collects butterflies: A "queer duck," they say, if they actually meet one. "Either a monstrosity or a fool," some might allow. How strange it is these same people read the books written by just such nocturnal troubadours, use words they've coined—and ideas—yet, commonly treat unknown poets with dismay.
One thing is clear to me, there are many midnight poets in the world.

Dwight R. Droz
Scandia Patch

DINING AT MITZEL'S

I recently stopped at a fine Poulsbo restaurant I often patronize. (The food is excellent.) Our waitress, Patricia, a comely lass, reminded my wife and me of a girl named Grace. At that time our daughter and Grace attended Central Kitsap High in Silverdale before the mall-and-wall-to-wall arrived. Back then it was a valley of farmsteads and streams. Grace had an infectious laugh with a generous stash of *bonne-vivant* humor.

Patricia hands us a menu. We chat a moment. I order clam chowder and a half-sandwich. Pauline orders a soda and snack. After a few more words, I venture this remark, right out of the blue and off the cuff, "I think you either can or should write." (That's a guess, as usual, but it gains some quick response.)

"Well," she replies, "I recently had an unfortunate experience; so I wrote a poem. After I composed those verses, I put them in an unusual place."

I ask her if she has a copy. She holds it up in an eye-wink, a single page.

I scan it briefly, feel new interest jelling.

I know its asking a lot," I say. "This poem's unusual; I'd prize a copy if one's available."

She's pleased. "We've a copier; why not?"

When our order is ready, the comely waitress plans to deliver the poem. Fact is, things grow quiet for a moment on that drowsy afternoon; so Patricia declares a quick break to sit with us. She reads the poem and her voice vibrates with immense concern over this "ever-repeating" memory of her sister's demise.

The world is chock full of stories, and here's one more to prove it—one I never ever expected to write.

The grim twist is, she wrote the poem to bury it!

When Patricia's children have grown up, I hope she keeps jotting notes. This is the poem she penned on the fatal day of her sister's demise:

When I first found out, all I wanted to do
    was scream and shout!
That devastating feeling I had inside was so strong,
    I had to ask myself, "What happened?
        What went wrong?"

From that point on, is when I started to long
    for my sister to be next to me.
I closed my eyes and I pictured her smile,
    her laughing, full of life and full of glee.

Then I knew that this could never be,
    because this is what they call reality.
I took a deep breath, then let out a sigh,
    and that's when it hit me, I started to cry.

The tears I cried are asking God "Why?"
    "Why did she have to die!"
The pain that she left for all of us,
    has made me full of anger and disgust.

Eva, we never got the chance to say
    that we all love you and that it will be ok.
Just give it your all, fight and give it one last "Try."
    Then you left us and you didn't even say
        "Good-bye!"

The tears that I have already cried are from the heart
    and the intense pain I felt deep inside.
The tears that I'm crying is my way of saying,
    "I forgive you,"
Considering all that you've been through,
    and to say, "Eva, I love you, and now it's time
        to say Good-bye!"

Patricia Bates (August 4, 1995)

Patricia placed this poem in Eva's casket; death was termed a suicide. She was only 38. We wish to honor the author, a working waitress who deserves a writer's wreath!

Mitzel's, managed by a most gracious restaurateur and dear friend, George Comeau.

Note: March 26, 1999. No attempt was made to edit the writer's poem written in deep emotional stress. To do so would be a breach of trust.

The Kite Fliers

A GIRL WITH CORN-TASSEL HAIR

Chapter I

In sunny southern Idaho where the fields roll smoothly to the margins of the broad desert, a narrow road goes marching past the lane of tall poplars as it wends upward to the juniper-clad foothills. It is a dusty byway lined with ragged Russian thistles where blue lupines flame beneath rusted barbwires that sag and saunter carelessly along the sage-strewn barrow pits.

As you wander down this mile of quiet lane, a chortling stream will meet you whose sole intent is to race you to the willow grove where, like a laughing scamp, it runs away to hide in floods of yellow clover field.

Prose alone does not enable me to tell the story of this mile of lane and of the "little people" who roamed it—like a girl who romped here, whose hair always reminded me of this poem:

She was one of the corn tassel maids
That linger in books and sunny-brook shades—
Reminds you of picnics and spiced lemonades,
Romps through meadows and bright Autumn
      glades.

    She lived in a fine house overlooking the river. Mourning doves called through the afternoon, and a river breeze teased the poplar leaves by the porch.

SUE

It is evening in the valley
   at the bosom of the hill
Where purple shadows wander:
   the evening breeze is chill.

I can hear some coyotes calling
   on knolls across the way,
And desert thrushes singing low
   at closin' of the day.

Cricket time is chummy here
   in hedges by the wall,
As sleepy sparrows chirp-a-lirp
   in the rustic poplars, tall.

From high on Harrison mountain
   where high piled snow banks lie,
A lowing Hereford poses,
   silhouetted on the sky;

Aspen groves lie quiet
   a hush about them streams,
As my thoughts, like papers rustling,
   turn to fancy, golden dreams.

The mourning cloak is nestled
   to the willow's leafy bough,
As a creek makes throaty murmurs
   to the jingling of the plow.

The horses hurry homeward;
   they're tired, but quicken pace.
The milkin' cows come plodding in
   with slow and languid grace.

And the heavy air is heady,
   where apple blossoms cling,
As Susan with the drinkin' pails
   goes, whistlin' to the spring.

She's standin' at the meadow gate,
   and waves as I drive through.
I call and toss the lines to her
   in a bonnet starched and blue;

So happy that I'm comin' by,
   she's such a friendly pal;
I laugh and tweak her nub-of-nose—
   that freckled, corn-haired gal!

She's got a face that's a cameo chase,
   red lips that smile so cute!
A mass of "glinty," yellow curls
   and freckled cheeks to-suit!

And tiny wisps of laughter,
   a-wrinklin' 'round her eyes,
With a fond breeze whippin' after
   like some goddess of the skies!

And when she laughs, it makes you think
   of creeks that burst from snow
In freedom lovin' meadow glades
   where pale-eyed daisies grow.

She's slender as a willow rod
   and stands so neat and slim;
Wearing a dress of gingham-press,
   with ruffles at the rim;

She's the slender sort of beauty
   whose complexion needs no veil—
Not a girl whose always primping,
   not the slender sort that's frail—

But a girl whose charm and manners
   seem to well from hidden springs,
Who walks as if her slippers
   were endowed with hidden wings.

Now, bless you, she's no slaver,
   and she's not a menial shirk;
If she has one blessed *failing*—
   it's love of honest work:

But if you, by way of pity,
   think her life's a weary chore,
Just listen to her, laughing there—
   she's happy to the core!

A girl who walks out daily
   in fields of sun and shower;
Who searches all the meadows o'er
   for rosebuds in their bower.

Her arms are strong as hempen lines
    from stacking summer sheaves—
Her ears attune to poetry
    of whispering poplar leaves.

Some may prefer the city girls
    of frail and tailored looks,
The kind who trot to concerts
    or choose "best-seller" books,

A dainty flower of "social sets,"
    linguistic in her drawl—
But a little gal in gingham
    is the sweetest of them all!

Yes, you may wholly disagree,
    but if you'd like a pal,
I hope you find one half as nice
    as that freckled, country gal.

Chapter II

    Do not confine that mile of lane to any factual measurement—in my mind it reached from infinity to reality. On the far-western end of it lay a mystery of horizon's and golden sunsets from whence came winds that conversed for days on end among the swaying poplars. At the far-eastern end of it lay home, definite and secure.

    There was no need to travel farther for it was an intrinsic scale of the whole universe, and so it is even today. It is my definition of being—of continuing existence—of beginning and end. I seek its simplicity.

It reached much farther, figuratively, than its narrow mile, for the associations linked with it swept far beyond. At its end lay a trail leading to an old Indian campsite on the banks of a river where we spent many happy hours searching for arrowheads along a sandy bluff.

South of it resided the sleeping hamlet of Declo; northward rose snow-capped vistas where the saw-edged ridges of the great Sawtooth Range stood in bas relief on clear winter days. They were possibly seventy-five or eighty miles beyond us.

Yet, there in that spot was the axis, the nucleus of living and experience. One step beyond that mile, it seemed there was a difference in the very resilience of the earth—still familiar ground, to be sure, but the sharp edge of familiarity was blunted. The horses knew it when they turned the corner of that mile of lane. The cows, stupid as they sometimes seemed, nevertheless had a certain air of "savvy," when we hazed them around the fence corner, that home was the object set upon, and a straw barn, a refuge indeed, with hay to fill every manger.

How easily the lark adjusts himself to every mood of earth and sky just as his somber brown wings blend to the shadow and color of the earth he loves. As we roamed in the wheat stubble or stacked the bright sheaves behind whirring mouths of greedy binders, the meadowlarks sang for us their songs of plenteous harvests.

Those unquenchable brown birds with the souls of angels loved our companionship as they floated up to render their arias no operatic score can surpass. No pompous conductor standing with upraised baton on some imposing podium ever delivered his melody from a host of instruments with more ease or simplicity than this winged and living flute. Poised on the rusted barbwire, nonchalantly loafing as we jostled with the heavy headed sheaves all through the long, hot August afternoon, I hear again this challenging vagabondish melody ringing:

THE CHORISTERS

How can there be a sweeter song
Than choirs of larks upon the mead,
As, winging in a choral throng,
In some wild melody they lead
That beats upon the autumn air—
What greater rhapsody is there?
A classic lyre, a pastoral flute,
A shepherd singer is as mute
To that rare wealth of songs profound
That ring where golden grain is bound.

Note: Old radio copy, originally written in the 1930's. Read on several radio stations.

TO A FRIEND
(Florence Brahms)

If ever with the passing years I find,
In brief communion with *some deeper sense,*
That I have grown no wiser in my mind
And creep upon my age with penitence:
What shall I do, if all this poverty
Has shut my longing soul to Beauty's cry
Till only distress in all things I *see,*
Till Beauty vanishes and fancies die?

When I, in such state, find my soul so obscene
That I no longer heed when bird notes ring,
Nor revel in the hillside's tender *green,*
When grasses roll above it in the spring;
When I have come to doubt all earthly things,
The *very* God whom worshippers descry;
When I have come to scoff the power of kings
In seeing all things wasted, all things die:
A spirit sweet as thine will solace me,
Though but a memory of the treasured past,
Restoring to *my* soul's infirmity
Sweet visions of the Beauty it has lost.

Note: The poem "To A Friend" was written when I was about 21 or 22. After my father died on the farm near Declo, southern Idaho, I drove to Arizona to conduct my mother and sister to a new environment on advice of my brothers who left the care of survivors to me. My sister, Dora, a teacher, had been ill and was recovering from scarlet fever (I believe that was her illness). My brothers thought mother and Dora needed the warmth of an Arizona sun. It was my job to see they got it.

We settled in Phoenix in the front of a camp where poor Arkansawyers and other escapees of the depression were congregated in small, converted vans, trucks with canvas campers, small tents and shabby cabins in the rear of the large campground. The desert was all around us sprinkled with saguaros, ironwoods and ever-present mesquite whose leaves tilt sidewise in the hot sun making scarcely any shade at high noon.

I lived in the best part of the camp on Van Buren Avenue. We had a small house trailer. I attended Gregg Shorthand School in February and March. There was a beautiful, poetic and impressive girl who had a limp due to polio of some ancient time. I was impressed by her and wrote this poem; as I have so often stated in other writings I was not inclined to go with girls who were crippled only because two cripples do not make a good match. I firmly believe this, but I really admired that girl training to be a stenographer. She had lovely brownish-gold hair. Fine features and a bubbly disposition. I wrote this for her encouragement. We were good friends at the school. She did have a suitor also attending there. I spent much of my typing practice time writing poems and an essay now and then.

THE FORSAKEN BOUGH

Look out upon that lone, forsaken bough
Where once the plaint of doves in echo beat
Against the quiet eve: How saddening now;
The gray sod gapes with wound of prying ice;
Where wind and famine spread their avarice
The prying snow stacks up its bitter hoard,
Lovely and desolate in winter rain;
Yet beauty still doth linger here and there
Where lifeless blossoms freckled with the snow,
Slow sinking, dying—gleaming softly—glow
In memory o'er the naked fields of past
Where, filled with blust'ry rage, up flies the blast.
Still do we feel some refuge hidden from sight
By today's grief where late did joy alight,
A frail and fragile wing did hover here
On this dry stalk of milkweed pod; and there
Will lift the crocus of some springtime fair.

And each doth from the winter gales exact
Some duty and some privilege to keep
The beauty of that bygone youth intact
Where the portcullised stalk of rosebush sleeps,
Half-naked, where the wind has pried the snow
Yet left the vague remembrance where they grow.

Thus, dear one, though this bitter loss I feel
That thy dear form hath fled the mortal bier,
And left but ravaged memory of the year
Of Death, yet where that gray mound rises with a cross,
Battling the blast, the feeling is not loss.

For Winter and the vanguards of her pack
Cannot shut thy thought forever back,
Or into realms forgotten ever press
Beleaguered memory unto bitterness.

Note: Written following death of my father in the 1930's. Copied from yellowed sheet almost illegible as I write.

THE GREATEST GIFTS

The greatest gifts of life are not received,
    but only half attained and touched with sorrow.
As faintly shared as breathes a winded flower,
    as scarcely touched as any spattering shower
That droops the careless grass until tomorrow:
    the greatest thoughts of men are unretrieved.

The love is grandest which is unattained,
    faintly sweet with sorrow and unsaid;
Muted with past joy, by tears unlaved,
    those inward woes by reticence enslaved
Yet fill the soul with pride for tears unshed;
    the greatest good may come from good ungained.

Yet, fancy holds us all unto her grasp,
    and steel nor iron shall outwear our dreams.
Such is their inmost strength that men forbear
    to creep in nothingness of light and air,
But bathe their hurt in fancy's shaded streams,
    and speak but with their eyes and firm hand clasp.

Note: Letters "abccba" indicate the rhyme pattern used in each of three verses of this poem. Line one rhymes with line six, line two rhymes with five, and three and four form a couplet in the center of each verse, a distinctive pattern. (Written December 1941.)

RETURNING

Don't call me a friend; dwell on forgetting.
    I'll never know if I caused you to cry.
I'll never say I loved you, or ever
    will ask you to shed a tear when I die.

Shower your love, your favored affection,
    on others, new-chosen, more favored than I.
The memories I cherish are locked in my breast;
    and no thief will gain them, for all he may try.

I thought of you often as years hurried by;
    sunny days, ocean sprays, a bright summer sky.
Catkins on willows. Boat rides on billows,
    onward, and dawn-ward, Snake River flows.

Don't call me a friend. I will not allow it!
    Such feeble "good faith" just poisons my soul.
Pay me no mind; speak of me never.
    Old-loves like these are feeble and droll.

I seldom relate, "We were often together."
    I don't beg for favors when I am oppressed.
But deep in my heart I'll love you forever,
    till memories from childhood
        dissolve in my breast.

This rambling rose that duly grows
    upon a swaying spray,
Will find but thorns and thistles, now,
    where blossoms bloomed in May.
        I'll be on my way.

WITH WEARY HEART

I looked upon the world with weary heart
And said, "In all things imperfection lies;
Nature's too diverse in all her art;
Little, 'wearing-troubles' cloud my eyes."

I saw no beauty in the ushered dawn
That lit the desert-drabness of the hill:
I said, "The beauty of old years is gone;
Why is this heart so mute—the soul so still?"

I saw no beauty in the world—until, one day,
I spied a lark with wings of solemn gray
Pressing her breast against a windswept lea;
I heard her song! And I was free!

I thought the world a dull, a drab place
And then I saw a baby-face—laughing at me!
I found scant joy in snows piled high,
Black clouds at eve, cold winter sky
That reddens with falling dusk: yet, now I see.

For I thought my heart was mute—
    and then, one day,
I watched a blind violinist play
"A Melody of Hope." And I was free!

Note: Used on a weekly radio program "The House by the Road," at Station KIDO in Boise Hotel, a Southern Idaho broadcaster in the 1930's.

IN TWENTY YEARS

When twenty years the snows have come
To grace the mountain high,
And far above the valley gleam
Against a winter sky,

Will I enjoy the fragrant flow
Of the forest's windy breath
Or lie beneath the banking snow
Reposed in arms of death?

Where future years may guide our feet
We question not for long
Who feel the constant hours beat
Unto the close of song;

And yet the question does repeat
In fears that will not go.
Where will I be in twenty years
When falls the winter snow?

Note: I believe I was a student in Declo High School when I wrote this, around 1929 or 1930.

THEN AND NOW

A little lad who used to play
For all the mellow summer day
And tossed white pebbles in the pool
And tagged the ripples off to school.

A growing boy who stacked the sheaf
And swung the sickle wide and free
And saw the sunset with belief.
"O, lad! O, youth! Come back to me!"

> The echoes ring far down the years,
> The red suns fade, the stars grow dim—
> And old man pushing back his fears
> Calls down the lane, "Come home now, Jim!"

> The echoes roll along the caves
> Of lava at the garden's close
> And blossoms out in creekside rows
> Of poplars tossing by the waves.

> The creek purls by, a litany;
> And soon s shrill young voice replies,
> "'Tis I, grandfather—coming! See!"
> Far down the orchard lane he flies.

A barefooted lad like a bounding deer
With tattered shirt and head ablaze
With thatch that tosses in the breeze—
Again one little lad stands here.

A little boy who loves to play
For all the mellow summer day
And tosses pebbles in the pool
And tags the ripples off to school.

30

LOVE UNREQUITED

Don't call me a friend; forget me forever!
I will not know if it costs you a sigh,
I will not prate that I loved you or ever
    coax you to shed cold tears when I die.

I will not say, "We were often together":
Or beg for your favor, though I am oppressed.
But, deep in my heart, I will love you forever,
    till warmth of the spirit grows cold in my breast.

Call me no friend. O, let me endeavor
That the past sheds its fruit of joy and of pain.
I ask for release, and speak of me never,
    for joys of old days cannot live again.

The dawn in its beauty, refulgent with splendor,
Stars, warm rains, the bright summer sky:
All these dear things you may well remember,
    but waste no fond pity on one such as I.

Far better, my dear, to dwell on forgetting,
Press unto sleep old beauties that fled.
Vain is the sigh, and vain's the regretting of sweet
    childish rapture when friendship is dead.

Yet, in your thoughts, a shadow may linger—
A tie left unbroken, a fond memory pressed:
I do not ask you to harbor the stranger,
    to leave it, disarmed, lie asleep in your breast.

Share no vestige of me; you should not allow it!
For feeble good faith but poisons my soul!
Dwell on new friends—I cannot endure it that ought
    I once shared looks redundant and droll.

Shower those smiles, your favorite affection
On others more pleasing and worthy than I.
These memories I treasure are in my protection,
    and no thief will gain them for all you may try.

THE KITE FLIERS

The children are flying their kites today;
    the March wind is rattling panes.
I think of days when we used to play
    with kites in the windy lanes,
When clover beds, like "windbound" seas,
    tossed under a cloudy sky
In the wild, sweet scent of a meadow breeze
    where lilacs blossomed by.

The poplars, plumed with bursting buds,
    on hill and valley ran
With music riots from the floods
    of larks in caravan.
Where wild sweet clover filled the glade
    along the broad canal,
The wild bee plied his busy trade
    with noise-some madrigal.

The blackbird flashed his ebon throat
    above the bright stream's flow;
And crickets sang an endless note
    along the orchard row,
As over lanes—and poplars, tall—
    the bright-hued kites we flew.

Above the highest of them all,
    like specks among the blue,
Might my thoughts thus surmount the skies
    above life's empty halls
And, with that childish joy, arise
    o'er barriers and walls!

The children are flying their kites today.
      the wind is a rollicking fool—
And just the fellow with whom to play
      on rushing out from school.
And you who watch them through the pane,
      are you so weary, or blind,
           as to think their frolic is all-in-vain.
Or have you a kite to mind?

Note: Written one March day in the 1930s for radio broadcast. I believe I read this over a Twin Falls Station. Was it KTFI?

MOUNT HARRISON

I look on yonder snowy peaks
And feel the mount and I are each alone,
I, in a world of men,
The mount in a realm of stone.

O, I have felt the chill winds breath,
Have faced the late Autumn's frosty death,
And shared the chills of friendships lost—
Alike the ravages of frost!

And when the sun has swept it clear,
My soul has sung its beauty here,
Or wept, alike, in floods of rain
When mists envelop mount and plain.

O! I've seen grassy tides in June,
Enveloped by one summer's moon,
And felt wild tumult in my breast!
I wished my heart could find its rest

Among the quaking-aspens, red.
But when upon it leaves have shed,
Or brooks grow thirsty in the heat
Where, merciless, the sun has beat,

I feel we two are friends—and each alone:
I, in a world of men;
The mount in a realm of stone.

Note: One of my earliest poems, written when I was twelve years old. The high peaks of Mount Harrison were full visible to the south of us. It remains ever in my mind.

THE PERISCOPE OF TIME

Being a precocious kid of nine or ten has foibles and benefits. Looking back at age 86, I look as through a periscope plumbing waste waters of time. Now, I spot one distant memory of a Denver Post Sunday Section with cartoons of an earlier day.

It's December of 1921.

That afternoon as I read the comics, I am lying on a blanket on the lawn swatting ferocious flies and stomping ants with my fist.

Here, among the Cosmos, flowers universally known, waved white blossoms. I cannot find their name in a current issue of Jung's Seed Catalog. We called those flowers by the Cosmos Ragged Sailors. They looked like this little sketch made long ago:

Bachelor Buttons also blossomed here. There, were other blooms with bright, black buttons gleaming. We loved Holly Hocks; who could forget them? Pansies peered with a clown's faces in those lava rings. Precious things! My sisters picked our simple posies for Sunday School in Declo.

Farmers had little time for pretties. Dad tolerated flowers to please mother who tended a garden filled with raspberries, strawberries and currants with those vines of tiny grapes. What wonderful treats!

Back to the theme of my memory. There on a quilt lies the Denver Post. I'm batting flies. Mosquitoes love this resting spot threading under the poplars. Gnats share this grass and blanket, though not invited. Ants scramble across it—grim-mouthed rebels. Scissors wave hopefully in those fierce, red jaws.

That's how it was.

Flat on my tummy, ignoring ants and their rants, I study that marvelous newspaper Sunday Edition, fluttering in a warm Idaho breeze. The comic section's big; the print's large and sprawly.

Look at Slim Jim and the Force. He's skeletonic-hoodlum, always running from the police. He cabooses from the Force in every issue. Cartoonists of those days didn't worry much over story content. No need to play it again, Sam! Naaw! Just Draw it again, George.

Same thing's true of Jiggs. He's usually sneaking off to Dinty Moores' on every Sunday spread. Of course he has to get out of the house, just like boys do. He's got a tough job, eluding Maggie's watchful eye.

This skit was specifically drawn for Irishmen; nevertheless, all immigrants from the slack-coal yards to those bountiful-boulevards loved "Bringin' Up Father" as much as the New York Irish clans did.

Maggie's rollin' pin's always cocked as Jiggs nimbly wire-walks the high-powered electric lines to Dinty's digs? Hope the insulation is sound.

Once inside Dinty's place, fat cigars and cold beer mugs soon make Jigg's nose glow red. He loves corned beef and cabbage at Dinty's Nest and Bar. Har! Har! Jiggs was a magnet for all his drinkin'-an'-gamblin'-kin.

>Some wore spats and spiffy cravats;
>Loafers and chauffeurs—those old alley cats.
>Such types were bad, made Maggie mad.
>Dreams of high society, nearly drove Mag bats!

In comic piers, it ran for years,
Sans major change or minor cheers.
Maggie kept her hair in a bun;
While Jiggs remained an oafish one.

A city man's comic,
A country man's scoff.
It took a generation
To cool readers off.

Remember comedy skits, after the main feature of a twenties movie? Keystone Cops skittered across Hollywood Landscapes in the early day flickers. Remember: "Our Gang Comedies," Alfalfa and his friends. Freckles on his face remain forever-trends. Slim Jim was always running from the Force. Cartoon characters were blithely unwise, ranting about a point-zero-four Richter-ish sort of disguise.

Slurps like Ol' Slim Jim raced through alleys and fireplugs. Jim hid behind old garbage cans, avoiding cops and drags. Hiding in gigs or livery rigs, his spirit never lags. Like Happy Hooligan, a tin can on his head, he fled—all dressed in rags.

O! Don't forget kind Chester, Gump, you must admit he was a chump—had a big nose—a nothin'-chin. So people laughed; a jest is no sin!

Those were the days of Rin-Tin-Tin. As ya know Rinny was a dog. Now sell me a ticket and a good hot dog.

Vaudeville brought comic Harold Lloyd, the timidest lump on celluloid, with inch thick glasses an cool straw hat—at the Bijou Show house—is where he's at.

A fumbling, bumbling hick-baboon. Harry couldn't carry a tune; couldn't charm a dame or earn a dime. But we loved Harry all the time.

The coppers never caught Slim—never, ever! We thought he was salubrious-and-funny. Repetition was desirable as the movies made their money. Heart-throbs and sleazy slobs. Swedes from snowy realms, every bloke would spend his poke to see movies with Richard Barthelmes.

One more comedy strip now comes to mind. Ten-year-olds admired Hairbreadth Harry, a Sunday page special. We loved it! There was—O, Curses! A villain! His aim was to foil our hero. Old rock-solid "Hairbreadth" what a name! Now the villain in charge was a monster whose true moniker escapes me entirely, sad to say.

That villain had long, hairy legs, a stingy mustachio; he wore tight black pants and a frock coat sorta like those an undertaker wears. He is bad news every week in the Sunday Comic section.

Today's scene covers a race track. Hairbreadth Harry, our hero, is bound to always win; but that skulking crook, we just mentioned, about seven feet tall, wearing a black suit, plans to beat Harry in the race and win a gold cup.

Do you spot him skulking in the bushes by the track? The plot, or the pot, if you prefer idioms, is boiling merrily here.

Yes, that's Hairbreadth Harry juicing his Hupmobile Eight around the last bend. He's in the lead. But a villain is lurking, working hard to change the tale.

That Villain's a treacherous, slob, with droopy mustache curls on his upper lip and fancy black boots on his tootsie-woots.

He has a rotten, cheatin' driver hired for the plot. With a Cannonball Flier foaming fumes around the spot. Ten pistons ringed for Caliente; the Cannonball is splitting flames—a beast of 1920. It cost ol' Villain plenty dough for a crook from desert trails. He forfeits bail or breaks out of jail; and hates Gringos intently.

He could never beat our Harry if the race was fair and square. But these are guys that we despise who cheat and just don't care.

Harry's in the lead. Villain's hireling's close behind; cussing the dust that Harry flushed—and served it up in kind.

Last lap at last. The race is fast. Look there! Villain's sprinkling tacks when Hairbreadth Harry steers his rig, a hero can't re-cast. Villain's always up to tricks; he did 'em in the past.

Old Hairbreadth's back wheel is thumping. It's true the tire's flat. It's too late for pumping. What will he make of that? Off rig, he hops, appalled and stunned; then grabs ol' Villain by his cummerbund.

"Villain!" hollers he. "Yer due some pay! Ya gone too far, damaged the car. Revenge is on the way!" He grabs skinny Villain with one big paw; wraps him on a flat tire from brisket to the craw! He fits on the tire like covering a mall. Ol' Villain wraps around the rim like a bouncy ball. He ties Villain's laces over the rim. A cowlick and a mustache are the best you make of him. Harry's fires up, revs speedily on the turn.

The way he hacks a track makes his red eyeballs burn. Beats every racer by a thin eyebrow.

AND...
    Harry is the winner,
        From a slow beginner!
            Wow!

Chitchat

PARTY CHITCHAT

Introduction

Have you ever been to an office party where a very mixed group attempts animated patter, jousting for a place in the limelight. I've attended many of these. When the event is about to end, nearly every member attempts to utter something singular and "epical" as they exit with a bow. Sometimes a thoughtful misfit, while balancing a glass and half-sandwich on his knee, attempts to record such an event for posterity. Here's about the way it goes.

Guest Number One
"You may have met inventor Bell
Whose miracles we know so well!
We'd tell you more about it—but
Pure Science does run rather *Rut*!"

The simple fact this goes to show
Is: "Pardon, but I soon must go;
My ex-wife came with a boxing-beau—
I really have to scoot, you know!"

Guest Number Two
You may have heard of Pastor Yates—
"A paragon of classic dates,"
Say all the suitors that he hates.
(He thinks they all are reprobates!)

One salient truth this act deplores
Is: Monkeys travel on all fours.
People cavort on only two.
Those monkeys get bananas too.
(I wish that mine were free! Don't you?)

Guest Number Three
Next on the scene is Lucia Lush
Imported from the Hindu Cush.

When L. L. picks someone for a go,
"Look out; take care! Yo-Yo!"
This gal has no "so-ci-o!"
Her polka is uniquely skewed;
On top of that, this gal is rude!

So don't be surprised if I leave;
I got some catsup on my sleeve;
I feel weak, and I'm short of sleep
Because I'm always counting sheep.
They ba-ah! and blat! I roll the sheet;
At breakfast I can hardly eat.
So don't expect me to be funny—
And I didn't bring any money—
A sorry-bunny!

Guest Number Four
Ah, there he is, a matador;
One type you never met before:
"Yes, indeed! He is a bore!"
With bull-tight trousers, skinny shanks.
Would I like to meet him?
"Well, no thanks!"
I didn't curry Arafat!
And this charade's a pool-a-splat!

Party Numero Five
You've heard of her, Maybella Swinch.
A face and torso fit to pinch.
That gal devours one ham for lunch;
And gobbles grapes up by the bunch.

M's very good at throwing shot
Say all the lifters 'round she brought;
Nobody wants her for a steady gift,
Not even the guys who work swing shift!

Party number Six

There is a chap named Gorbus Schwag.
A banker who's too prone to brag.
He only owns two bags of gear;
(Bankers are sometimes "tight," I fear.)
Shares rent with teller, Du-Le-Lier.

It's evident there's something strange—
But, pardon, I must leave the range!
An old, ex-date just joined the show.
(I think I'll exit tippy toe!
My bicycle runs very slow.)
It will seem rude of me, I know!

Note: This was initially written 30 or 40 years ago. Like long stored cheese, it finally ripened into a snack for between 10 and midnight. Owls are out; curs are yapping. Just a snicker between catnapping.

NILEAN CAPERS

The "croc-a-loc-a-doc-a-dile"
Is a most astute reptile
Who proudly sports a beaming smile;
This schmool might fool you for awhile!

While squat ten-footers dot the Nile
Or flounder up the Tigris,
This crock seems bigger by a mile,
And unknown to the bibliophile.

I'm rather vague as to his taste,
But this much I do remember.
When he has chomped you at the waist
And severed your suspender,
    Point one: He acts with dubious haste;
    Point two: The teeth aren't tender!

A polyglot of curious folks
Hop off the bus to greet 'em.
Old folks and blokes in jobish-cloaks
Rent ten-buck stools to seat 'em.

Every tourist oohs and ahs
When wacky crocks unlock their jaws!
Just hear those ripples of applause,
So different from "tame" Santa Claus!

Once a tourist, gone-and-now-forgot,
He chose to linger by this spot.
Next day, ignoring a warning sign,
Pitched tent near waves at half-past-nine.

Was this dude brave, naïve or simple?
He basks his toes in the saltless brine.
One hour bonged, a crock looked on—
    The last time we saw Wimple.

In ripples, less than two feet deep,
It still is dangerous water!
I know I won't dip in there soon,
And I don't think you aught'er!

THE HAVEN

"Grasshopper, grasshopper,
    where will you go?
The scarlet leaves wither
    and down falls the snow!"

"Butterfly, butterfly,
    where can you hide?
Wild storms choke the meadow
    with ice far and wide."

"I will go to the lands
    where spent Summer flies,
Where God spreads His table,"
    Grasshopper replies.

"And I," said the butterfly,
    "will slumber till June,
Snugly bundled away
    in my cozy cocoon!"

Question is: Winter had come. Remember Aesop's Fables? Do you think old grasshopper made it?

CHILDHOOD PLAYMATES

I searched for the friends in childhood I knew;
Those glad-hearted infants, how swiftly they grew!
Who rushed to the haymow in panic to play
Or frolicked a wind-harassed pasture land way:
Soft curls and freckles, blue eyes, demure,
Noisome and boisterous, quietly pure—
Pensively dreaming of names that I knew,
Sweet playmates of childhood, where are you?

Do you frolic some distant lane, drifted beyond
The dim conjuration of my childish wand?
Do you envision new flowers on far, windy lanes
Or chase yellow butterflies there on the plains
That stretch through the years—that part you from me?
My sweet, noisy children, where can you be?

Do you still seek the clover for rabbits we fed,
The daisies that toss in their wind-tumbled bed?
Are you searching a dove's nest or chasing a snake
Who skims the white waters that course the wild brake,
The crow in the willow, a lark in the mead,
A sweet-toned song sparrow who nests in the reed,
Some noisy kingfisher above the bright flow;
My sweet, noisy playmates, where did you go?

Note: Written in the mid-1930s for the radio show "The House by the Road," a weekly program for a Twin Falls radio station.

SUNBONNET BABE

"Sunbonnet miss, you're sweeter-than sweet,
    with tossing curls and dancing feet."
Her blue eyes glow as bright as a jewel.
    She's far too young to care 'bout school!

With innocent wiles and guileless mien—
    she's cute when messy, an angel when clean.
"Where are you going, my happy cherub?
    Don't you know, Babe, it's time for a scrub?"

Chasing butterflies down a garden path;
    frightened by a bumblebee's wrath.
Dancing up trails where the irises grow—
    as rambunctious as the rambling rose.

"You've little use for foibles or adult wiles,
    sweet sunbonnet babe,
        all laughter and smiles."

Note: Also written in mid-1930s for "The House by the Road." This miss roamed our neighbor's garden in Burley, Idaho. The next-door neighbor folks, whose little girl inspired this poem, were touched when they heard it read over the air; they said, "You can use our bathroom any time you wish."

THE LAMB PARADE

A small lad stands by the family gate
   as a sheep band ripples past;
The Idaho wind blows out of May—
   a wild, mischievous blast.

Silver June grass plumes all wave their wands;
   the scent of growing hay
Comes down the wind and warms the boy
   on this auspicious day.

The Matthew boys drive their sheep to range
   on the Cotterel hills each spring—
A tide of anxious mothers and bleating lambs;
   for a mile those echoes ring.

Two sheep dogs with red, lapping tongues
   race off to help their master:
They wheel and bark and scamper out
   to guide and move them faster.

The drover whistles and off they race
   like two wild clowns in motion;
O, how much he'd love to race with them,
   but his mind remands the notion.

Those long-limbed lambs nip clover buds
  or some wildflower cup:
That boy, enjoying a rollicking scene,
  prays this day will *never* stop!

How bright and yellow this wisp of trail
  where dandelions run.
A red-winged hawk soars overhead;
  his wide wings skim the sun.

Then, a good Basque shepherd arrives, bemused,
  with a crag-like, foreign face—
A soul who sees and understands
  the day,
        the boy,
              the place.

His left hand rattles a hoop of cans
  to stir the sheep forthright.
The face is wrinkled and weather-seamed;
  his locks are silvered white.

"Liddle boy!" he calls, as he signals an aide
  who is tracking close behind.
"Do ya wan-na lamb? Could you feed it, son?"
  "Yes, sir!" the boy opined.

His face beamed smiles as he stepped to the road
   in a glad-wappy state of mind.

Gone are the days of blackbird songs
   when wise winds ruled the mead.
My limbs grow weary. The Basque is dead;
   the world seems cold indeed.

I think, once again, of rushing waves
   of June grass tossing high:
Will I ever inhale that meadow's breath
   and perceive a child's blue sky?

It is strange! Though I strive to say it well,
   grown up words fail, by and by—
May the lads, who summoned our joyful days,
   never let the old dreams die!

The Book of Zoz

Hamilton Mill

by

- ZOZ -

<u>Forward</u>

At nearly ninety-one
      men and memories fade.
Sure wish I could find Oran
      and ride down the grade.
There's no dog to prance ahead,
      no rabbit bounding free.
The sage is all tilled under—
      and the plow is hunting me.

HAMILTON HILL

I'm draggin' a wagon
Up Hamilton Hill.
We're havin' a coastin' bee.
The grade is steep,
The dips are deep,
With grass as high as your knee.

A pheasant's crowin',
The wind's a-blowin',
Blue lupines toss a lot.
Wild sego lilies are hard to find—
But, on this hill, their *not*!

Sweet clover blossoms
Grow rank and sweet—
Busy bumblebees do their best.
This grass is soft as a big hayloft—
A wonderful place to rest!

It's like Heaven here
On Hamilton Hill,
Lazy-watchin' th' clouds drift over.
A playful breeze tickles
The back of my neck,
As grasshoppers click-in-the clover.

Our wagon is set
For a romp down th' hollow;
Here are the rules,
If your plannin' ta follow:

*"Never stand up!
Don't drag yer feet!
We don't baby sissies!
Ya needn't be neat!"*

You can just have fun
Like hogs hit a wallow!
So, fetch-up your wagon,
Hop in it and follow.

We don't allow girls here!
Their feet start-a-laggin';
And, sooner-or-later,
They'll break *any* wagon!

You know, the hill at Hamilton's
Really suits Oran an' me!
The grade is tight,
Those dips are deep—
That strip's a pip-peree!

That's Jim Hill Mustard
On the ridge;
Grey sagebrush sneaks behind it.
At the bottom, peeks
A three-plank bridge—
Yer lucky that ya found it!

Ol'Oran doesn't care
If we crash in the clover,
And Cubbie, his dog,
Just licks us ALL OVER!

We scramble to our feet!
Oran starts in a-jokin',
And we straighten-up our wagon
Just t'see what's broken!

Next, ya turn the rig around,
A headin' fer th' top,
Tuggin' our machinery,
And we're almost fit ta drop!

At last, we pile back on,
I grab ol' Oran's shirt,
And we go whizzin-down
In a cloud of goopy-dirt!

If a jackrabbit jumps out
On the bottom of a grade,
We just roar right on by 'im,
'Cause it's *ninety* in the shade!

It really doesn't matter
What lies in-wait today:
Old rocks, busted crocks,
Or a scoldy ol' blue jay
Hollerin', "*Oley, Oley Ay!*"

Note: As I gaze clear across nine-tenths of a century, I'm impelled to say how wonderful it was to know the Hamiltons and the Huntsmans. This tribute is long overdue. Hiram ("Hi" to his friends) always wore overalls; his capital was scant, yet this easy-going farmer was happy in solitude—a real pioneer! Hi was creative and he loved to repair old machinery. His favorite chore, for our benefit, was fashioning "new-born" wagons from old scraps. His kind wife made-do with no complaints: she sewed, canned, gardened, played the pump organ, and, tucked away in that lonely valley, resolutely fed her brood. The Huntsmans' had three children: Elaine, Oran and Willis. It was on Hi's wagons we coasted down Hamilton Hill. Near the desert, the lane to Huntsman's tarpaper-shack follows a ditch where sweet clover spews sugary scents and momma skunk marches plume-tailed-tots through lots of taut Forget-me-nots. Basso-bees hum some Straussian waltz, and nature thrives with happy lives.

ALGERNON OF PARIS

Once there was a Parisian named Maris
Who wheeled high, overalled, on a Ferris.
Caught his foot in a spoke. For a very bad joke,
On a cane, in the main, everywhere is.

He was lush, drank too much; what an eyeful!
Court patrons thought him a trifle;
Trashed his pants waste to knee
On a bit of debris. It was sightful.

Well, back to our hero named Maris;
Once greatest *Maitre'Dee* in all Paris.
Now, he coughs by the Eiffel,
Soaked in wine-skins and vinyl,
And lies on a park bench, supinol.

So, this plastered-in-Paris disaster
Proved 'im Destiny's tot and a master.
When he climbed, on a toot,
And spun on his boot, on a tall, obelisk-tic pillaster.

His foot slipped, he whirled like a caster
And he splat like an' antimacassar;
So I've run out of rime at a very good time;
But he hit the end even faster!

A rooby-dube-booby was Maris,
Who crashed there in rapt unawareness.
Now it's time for a pun. I can barely find one.
That's how they coined: "*Pil-ast-er of Paris.*"

THE FOUNDLING

Cantankerish and prankerish—in a Cotterel homestead glued—Chase had little time for fun when dry land tasks ensued.

Stop, it is time to plant one pin as a miniscule Muppet marches in! Essential to our story, in a tale that's truly-true, It gives me joy to toast this ploy—a mini-tale for you. The scene is Cotterel School.

    All during class, in high Junegrass,
        wild "jack-rabs" romp the yard;
    As large-or-mid, each settler-kid
        sees the ball ground cleared of shard.
    About this time, strange shifts entwine
        in Cotterel's remote vale!
    And then, a bit of history strides
        into this dusty swale.

Ellen (not her true name) was dumped by a cabin door; in a tiny crib came babe-and-bib, an orphan's-suit she wore!

Grump "C" seemes to bloom when this babe lights the room. When curious neighbors come to call, his wife finds that miss is "no trouble at all." The tot is such a sunny soul; they want her in spite of their scant bank roll. That house grows sunnier than it was in time past. Love roots have shoots designed to last.

So time drifts by. Gaunt settlers fry. It's clear good times are done. Gaunt gophers prowl; the burrowing owl returns to guard its run. Some settlers move near Rupert town, or spots of like renown…to Burley, "Twin" (or Po-ca-tello) where lokies smoke in hills dull yellow.

When my sister applied for a job one day, Acequian's hired her right away! She stayed with

"Ellen's" mom in a sand-swept "krall," long way out of Rupert—the school was quite small.

In due time, we go to visit May upon a lazy autumn day. Dad juices the Ford; down-dale it cabooses! That crate has the gait of a bumpous-caboosis! It's poppin' and crackin' the smoky old Liz! Dad's happy-and-sappy 'cause of Hallowe'en bizz!

> Ellen's pop had two cows he tended each day
> where we swung on a rope—
> a discreet hide-away.
> The hay smelled so fragrant;
> a breeze billowed through:
> O what a wonderful thing to do!

"El" was saucy, but happy to play in a farmer-charade on that marvelous day—secure with her pop and his blessed wife. This child was the gift that brightened their life, glowing with vim—and all gingham-gowned. She says "Mom will hem me new clothes as fall comes round."

> She wears pretty sweaters,
> Skirts high at the knee.
> I'll say she was pretty—believe-a-you-me!

May's busy teaching; I enter the room. "Studes" work in small spaces like four-lengths-of-a-broom. It wasn't bad, really. I'm framing a joke: "Don't 'miff' cubby-holes if the plaster ain't broke!" In a classical rash, one-roomed-school-teachers of those days defied present rules. No curtains seemed-needy to shelter the seats where students met Shelley or pontified Keats, plus Geography, History and Lewis-Clark feats.

Students tracked Oklahoma's mad race for new land, covered old "Indian matters" like Custer's Last Stand. Studied Chief Joseph 's battle on high Whitehird

Hill. That classic event is good history still. Finally, he drove a staff in the turf! "We will fight here no more!" He felt like a serf. The women are weary, all is disarray. Those exploits, so awesome, are still studied today.

While one class studies, another debates; there are few disruptions among these classmates. They're melded together—no one minds. At each graduation, you leave flowers behind and step into life serene and refined. May taught many years; still, she never forgot what a great class of students Acequia wrought.

Those kids were smart, I will attest. Each classmate counterpoints the rest. Every week, one lad feeds the pot-bellied stove. He jumps from studies, steps out in the yard, gathers more faggots and shakes the grate hard, re-sets the damper, hangs a poker on hooks, and then, without blinking, pops "back-to-the-books!"

This job was an honor—as best I could see. I'd love to "attend there!" I'd think, "Lucky me!"

Those maids and lads were fair-and-square! I met three at Albion, in two sessions there.

I roomed with (one) Acequian[1] at old Southern Branch who remembered young "Ellen," at Chase "H's" ranch. We talked of the Haruzas, and other folk about, remembering "Melvies" marble games. He shot those 'taws', choicest shooters, with clout!

"Teaching is tiresome!" some may say. But "sis" loved pupils—and they loved May! As for

---

[1] 'B' Valentine. We once batched together in Southern Branch. Bernie was an engineer who viewed my literary pursuits askance. Still, we were good friends. Then college was done, we met again at Puget Sound Navy Yard when World War II was hot-to-run. Now lieutenant on a Carrier, he invited me to dine. At the fete we remembered Acequia, and my sister he thought taught fine. Bernie was a pilot when he came home from the war. He flew a plane to Swan Falls to check their Power-Bar; it was there his plane abruptly fell—wherever he lies, I wish him well. A paragon of kindly men! Bernie, I hope we'll meet again!

"Ellen," dumped in Cotterel soil, kind parent's healed any vague turmoil.

> If the infant cried as mom combed her hair;
> Cuddled in a cradle-there,
> Watchful Chase would grossly blare!
> "Be careful!" Meek Mom complied.

I'm sorry that sweet lady eventually died! Her husband, domineering, never forgot that baseball gig—then, Fate traded his shot on a Major's lot; and he's plumped in a one-horse rig! All memories of his baseball clout died like a butcher's pig!

> When Ellen's mom and dad passed on
>   life no longer was a play.
> For a short time, she lived with us.
>   I think of her today!
> Please draw a final curtain
>   and end our Matinee.
> Most friends I "nouned" are under a mound,
>   and buried far away!

Note: The two Hruza (or Haruza) boys were named Melby and Melvin (or close to it). "Ellen," the unfortunate foundling, did not prosper after Chase and his wife passed on. I am not able to toss this episode in a trash barrel. I've too many roots in Cotterel and Acequia to cut a line. May ended her career in Topanga, California. She resides with my other sister, Dora, in a cottage on a bluff above the post office. Her home is near to "John Boy's" erstwhile Grandpa's estate. If this description seems obscure, let me hasten to add: "John Boy" acted in an old TV sequel with many repeats—now defunct.

Topanga is a quaint village, surreptitiously tucked in snide-lil'-hideaways of the Santa Monica Mountains—an old gathering spot for actors and notables of the Hollywood scene clear back to early flickers. Tarzans lazed here when out of work. Other wannabees, both real and non-authentic, displayed musculature quite brazenly among it's curvy-curly-coves. This quaint spot has a scary road the auto's love to battle as lofty peaks peer down on timbered groves and rich men's coves.

May, born in October of 1904, is now in her nineties. Yes, Acequia was her first assignment. It was there she bought Dolly, a black pacer, pictured in Volume I of my series *Culture On The Cuff*. I will never forget the tale of that foundling who cast her shadow in our lives. By the way, *acequia* is a Spanish reference to a "water ditch"—trust me. The settlement was near Lake Walcot at Minidoka Dam.

SICK-A-MUDDY

On the shores of Sick-A-Muddy
We are very buddy-buddy
Where the skies grow red and ruddy.
From our blanket now we toddle
To the stream to fill the 'boddle'
With a happy song we doddle.
Picking flowers by the basket,
We'll chop daisies if you ask it—
Even put 'em on your casket
      (just to mask it).

Though the fever here's atrocious
And the gators—most ferocious,
Not a good port for neurosis,
Or persistent halitosis.
If I only had the power
I'd be far-gone in an hour,
But we haven't beans or flour.
Our beater stabbed at dabs of fishin,'
But, alas, our hooks were missin'
      and the natives wound up kissin'!

So we're off to Timbuktu
With a whole lot drier view;
So good-bye—*guardez-vous*!
And a batch of "Toodleoos!"
Not quite Shakespeare, is it just prose
Fevered by miasmic flows
From the pen of D. R. Droz
On the 'hank-a-pankish-banks'
      of Sick-A-Muddy?

AN IMPERTINENT SERPENT

Does art, in part, let your heart un-coil
      with reading, writing—paints with oil?
Well serpents, who twine in the vinelands of toil,
      go reeling and writhing—and feinting-in-coils!
And this is my tenet: how my kettle boils!

I love Lewis Carroll—and *oysterly* stew,
      the carpenter, the walrus and oysters a-brew!
We all need confetti, I hope that is true.
      yes, this is my tenet: let's toss some to you.

How often a droll snake creeps into my day;
      persistent and obstinate, it won't go away!
A group of odd characters hove into view—
      unicorns and hunting horns now blare in revue.

Does this mayhem simply stem from how maids make
      the bed with pull-wooly comforters
          piled upon your head?
Droll poets, you know, are very slow to alert or inspire;
      a serpent, on the other foot,
          could cause lots of ire.
They'd abdicate their trundle bed like ants, pants a-fire!

Yes! This artistic snake with the sinuous coils
      keeps reeling and writhing—
          and feinting with oils:
That's good entertainment for barons-with-boils.

MOUNTAIN BOUNCIN'

Mountain Bouncin'

We drove to Vantage
 Washington
Not very long ago...
And all along the
 mountain pass
The cars fought
 toe-to-toe!!

And this was quite
 a trick—
 Because....

The air was thick
 with
 Snow!

Some tried to walk
    the banisters,
In spite of slippery snow...
And people, kids, and
    yipping hounds
Went flapping far below—!

Now, scenery is very nice.
This, no one will deny —
But who likes scenery upside down?
It's hardly worth the try.

In fact, I think
The most you'd see
Is stars
✦✧! ✦✧! ✦✧!
Not in the sky!

The snow kept falling....
Plip! and Plop!
In large........and juicy
Flakes....
We had no chains
Upon the wheels,
And did we get
The Shakes??

I'll say we did!.........
We drove-and-dodged,
We ducked, we dipped
   and wound;
While other cars were
   stalled on peaks,
And wrecks lay
   all around.

Not once — until
We made the flats,"
Did we feel Safe-
And-Sound!
We climbed out of
Our gas-machine
And hippity-hopped the ground:
We might have plopped
In some ravine
To not be missed
Or found!

Now, if I ever drive again
Where ice-capped summits glow,
It will be on a cross between
A yak and buffalo!

And I'll be wearing
Everything...
For 101° below—
Including chaps,
A set of traps,
And guides for
Crossing snow!

I once thought I was
         bold and brave,
But I get scared-and-
                  chill,
Whene'er I see an
            automobile
Come slurping around a hill.

From some high knoll
      I'll gladly wave
And wish them godspeed
       —when—
   I know I'm safely
       out of reach
   Of all gas-happy
         Men!

But if I be not brave or bold
  (As much you might suspect.)
Far better to grow ripe and old
Without my self-respect

Who wants to join the "noble dead"
Upon some snowbound hill,
Needs take no pains—
  (Just empty brains)
In a hopped-up automobile.

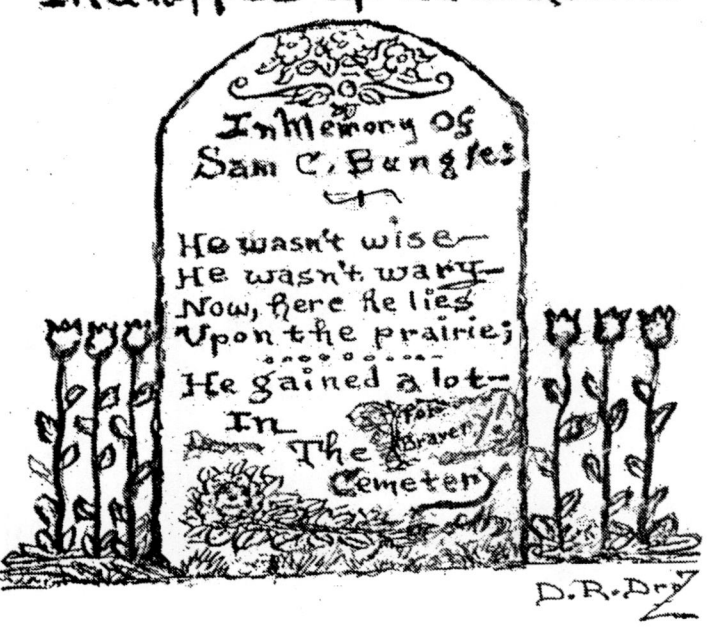

In Memory Of
Sam C. Bungles

He wasn't wise—
He wasn't wary—
Now, here he lies
Upon the prairie;
He gained a lot—
  In
The "for bravery"
Cemetery

D. R. Dry

THE TALE OF A PURPLE TIGER
by Zoz

This starts our play; so let me say,
A tigery tale is on the way!

Part I
MUFFINHEAD

*(Enter a Norwegian stable tender.
A primeval sort of chap.)*

One morning as the sun arose,
And the moon to rest was led,
I spied a Norse, on a dapper horse,
With a very-muffin head.
I seldom fib, in robes-and-bibs;
Yet, oft, I *lie* in bed.

This lad appeared,
He stroked his beard,
As to those about he cried:
"This pony's rare and debonair.
Prepare for a merry ride!"

The pony-track was busy-tack
As round-the-ring they rode—
By brat-kids and fat-nids,
Ol' pony's bod was bowed.

The Muffin Man, at close of day,
Cleaned the stable every way.
He served the trotter his favored tea.
How lucky can a pony be?

Muffin-Headed Man

That little horse was saucy.
His name was Herminfouth.
He had a spavin in the east
Plus ringbone in the south.
A very-handsome golden bit
Keeps-jingling in his mouth.

He's swamped with fancy trappings
From his shoulders to his knee,
Yet, I didn't like the haughty way
He stood and stared at me.

Next day, just when the sun arose,
As the moon to rest was led,
I spied this pony once again
Impatient to be fed.

A fancy saddle on his back
With silver conches shone.
I looked about. The groom was out,
And we two were alone.

So now I asked him pleasantly
Just where he planned to dine.
He gazed at me with a bitter eye
And spluttered with a whine;
"I cannot dine on oats!" he sobbed.
"My diet is *so* mean
That I can't exceed the calories
In a jar of Vaseline!"

Part II
PURPLE TIGER

A purple tiger sauntered up
From a grove of Jum-Jum trees.
He had green spats and ochre eyes,
With knee pads on his knees,
And looked so very-casual as
'Bout any old cat you please.

He fixed a very tender orb
Upon the pony there;
He did not wait for anyone
To offer him a chair—
The sort of chap who gets-along
Just about anywhere.

At last he heaved a cattish sigh;
"A diet," said he, "is sad!
I know all this, because, of late,
My diet's been so bad!"

"I have to watch my calories too,
Because my tail is long;
It does look terrible when too fat!
To be a pig is wrong!"
The little horse now bobbed his head
To prove he *went along*.

"I tell you what," the tiger gushed,
"I'll take you out to dine;
I'll buy you some pistachio cheese
And just a *snip* of wine.
And I will pay for everything,
If that's not out of line."

"I'd better not," the horse replied;
"Your tail is much too spotted.
I doubt you come of Plymouth stock:
I see your tail is knotted.
I doubt your diet has been lean.
Your stomach's much too potted!"

"Now, I comprehend," the tiger gushed,
"You're dolled-up. I'm *in shorts*.
This tends to make you critical;
I thought 'Bluebloods' wore sports."
Then, he heaved a "catty" laugh
And some derisive snorts!

"Very well—all right!" the pony cried;
"Maybe I was a fool;
I guess I'll go; you pay the bill;
I don't, though, as-a-rule."
The tiger growled, "Of course I'll pay."
He acted very cool.

"I've only eaten a zebra, small;
One hartebeest and a fallow deer;
And yet my stomach's rumbles
SO...
That I can scarcely hear!
I find, when I'm too hungry,
I've a tendency to *leer*."

Part III
THE PICNIC

"Well, come along," the tiger purred,
"It is *not* very far.
I know a lovely picnic spot
Behind a gravel bar."
At length they reached a grove of trees;
Not a cricket was about;
The pony, soon, was ill at ease;
This made the tiger pout.

"It's dinnertime," the tiger purred;
"Make haste or you'll be late!
I'd hate to catch you loitering
On our first dinner date."

Then, from his basket, neatly packed,
He picked a knife and hone;
Next, he unfolded a tablecloth
And spread it on a stone;
The last thing out was a massive plate.
Alas! He had but one!

Pony and Tiger Picnic — "There was only ONE plate!"

"Would you care for a menu?" tiger asked
As he poured a cup of tea.
"No need for that," the pony mused,
I think the menu is *me*!"

Part IV
MUFFIN DOG

Next day, the Muffin Man
Went walking a muffin mile
To find a muffin dog
That leaned upon a stile.

You see, this type of pooch
Is not a common Spitz.
A dog like this just mopes around
And sits, and sits—*and sits*.

But when it gets a scent,
If something that it likes,
It gets right off it's sitter,
Wags it's tail—and "YIKES!"

The man picked Towser up
And said, "Here is a scent.
Pray tell me what it is;
And tell me where it went."

He handed the dog a pony comb
And a bill for stable rent.
The little Spitz sat on it's mitts;
He *thunked* and *wherfed* and *whent*!

At last, he raised his head
And gave a puny "Yarp."
Ol' Muff' untied his leash;
They headed up a *garp*.

At first, they weaved a wood
And then, they swam a swamp;

It rained on them real-good;
O, what a lovely romp.

The Muffin Man said, "Spitz,
I hope you do not fail."
The pooch just raised his mitts
And pointed with his tail,

And there that tiger lay.
His spots looked very pale.
His clothes all needed pressing—
He'd fainted by the trail.

The Muffin Man got very sad
To think how pony died;
He saw a saddle lying there
And cried, yied and sighed.

But Muffin Men are smart!
And Muffin Men are quick!
He jumped upon that tiger's back
And tied him in a trick!
Ol' tiger never raised his head
Becuz he wuz so sick.

Part V
AN AWFUL FIGHT

Tigers are so very mean;
They should not be so crude!
Big wildebeests and antelopes
Aren't all the things they've chewed!

(Since ponies are for-riding—
They should *not* come unglued!)

The Muffin Man sat there and
thought
Under the Jum-Jum tree.
Said he, "That tiger never ought
To get away scott free!"

Old Muffin took the saddle
And cinched the tiger tight.
He swung aboard and yelled, "Let's Go!"
THERE WAS AN AWFUL FIGHT!

That tiger's spots popped off like corks,
He spluttered, coughed and swore—
And dove, tail-first into the stream;
The waves ran shore-to-shore.
But Muffin Man just waved his hat
And hollered, "Buck some more!"

The tiger finally lost his breath,
A shudder shook his frame;
A tear rolled from his ochre eye,
And he hung his head in shame.
He mentioned he was sorry
And acted very *tame*.

He coaxed, he begged and pleaded,
Till Muffin Man said, "WHOA!
You ate the transportation—
You've got to be the show!"
All the tiger uttered was,
"O, no! O, no!—*O, n-o-o-o-o-o-o*!"

"In addition," said the Muffin Man,
"There's more bad news today!
You must carry all the children;

And you can only nibble *hay*,
With oats morning-and-evening.
There is just no other way!"

"Tigers should not nibble people;
They shouldn't act so smart;
They should not be so thoughtless;
But have love in their heart!"

(If they won't do this by themselves,
We will have to *make them start!*)

This tiger learned a lesson;
He learned to live on oats;
He, now, *loves* little children,
And even nanny-goats!

So, if you go a traveling,
And spy a Jum-Jum tree,
Or bump a purple tiger,
Please take-a-ride for me!

TALES FROM LAMPLIGHT LANE

Tales From Lamplight Lane

The tall lamplighter
  Stalks alone.
    His boots ring on
      The cobblestone.

—

Whistling shyly, there he goes
By ivied halls through winding rose.

—

The torch casts shadows
  Down the street
And moonbeams glisten
  Around his feet.

—

The velvet shadows
  Creep behind
Trying to hide
  The lamp he minds.

The sun descends.
 The fireflies glow
Where shadows fall;
 The lamp is low.

The cricket fiddles
 Strike a tune
As poplars brush
 the crescent moon.

Now go to bed
 And close your eyes
As into misty dreams
 You rise
 Far over steeple,
  Pond and tree
  In Golden Isles
   Of "Never-Be."

From Africa
 To Sunny Spain
You ride a wild wind
 Home again
To wander back
 Through moor and lea
To haunted castles
 By the sea —
  Beside the murmuring sea.

The lamps glow brightly
   On Lamplight Lane
As bedtime comes
   Around again.

My mother tucks me
   In my bed
And waits until
   A prayer is said.

She smiles and winks
   In a special way—
"Read a story, Mother,
   Please", I say.

She opens *this* book
   And reads to me—
On Lamplight Lane
   Is the place to be!

She says, "Now, son,
   If you don't fuss
I'll read about
   Izzy after us."

The Izzyafterus

Izzyafterus
   Slips up the stairs
To try and trap you
   Unawares!

He's funny
   But, cantankerous.
He's old —
   And "riverbankerous."

He's very awkward
   In his travels,
Gallumping over
   Slippery gravels.

Is he submersible?
   More than a horse.
Is he reversible?
   Why, YES, of course!
It's hard to say
   which way he's going—
I doubt there's ANY
   WAY of knowing!

"Mama," I ask,
   "Is he after us?"
"Nonsense, dear,
   He's bluster and fuss!"

It's "Make Believe"
   On Lamplight Lane;
I'm not afraid—
   Please start again.

"Piffawiffs," says she
   with a clown-type face.
"This is ONE creature
   I just can't place!"

My mother turns a page to see,
And, afterward, she reads to me.

If you would like a closer look,
Now turn the pages of this book.

              To a Piffawiff

MEET A PIFFAWIFF

The Piffawiff
    Is just colossal!
He's very daffy
    Dumb, and docile.

It's fond of PEOPLE
    If they're edible;
And, once you meet,
    He's un-for-gedible!

Friend, have you seen
A Piffawiff?
I THINK I MAY HAVE
MET ONE,
IF —
THAT IS,
IT COULD HAVE BEEN
ONE,
BUT —
IT WORE A MASK
And walked a-strut
To hide it from
I don't know what.
SO —

If you see one
CALL ME!
Don't delay.
They're growing scarcer
Every Day.
YET —

Books ALL SAY
 The PIFFAWIFF
IS JUST A Granulated-Griff
 CROSSED with a
SMORGOUS BELL-VA-DUFF,
 And <u>that</u> description
  <u>IS ENOUGH.</u>

— MORE ABOUT "IZZY" —

The Izzyafterus
IS PROUD —
Though careful NOT
TO ROAR TOO LOUD

He loves corn soup
And pumpkin
Fritters,
And
Chases Cats
And —
BA<u>BYSIT</u>TERS!

THE THINGS LAMPLIGHTERS DO

In the evening after supper
   Mother tucks me into bed.
I peek out of my window
   To watch the lamps go red.

I can see an old lamplighter
   Every time I close my eyes
With golden torch a-burning
   And stardust in his eyes.

   When shadows creep
      Up Lamplight Lane
   Will my lamplighter
      Come again?

   His worn boots make
      The cobbles click.
   He whistles while
      He trims the wick,
   Pours the oil--
      Cleans the flue;
   These are the things
      Lamplighters do.

   He waves and nods
      As he goes by,
   A twinkle in
      His impish eye.

   A smile lights up
      His weathered face;
   He has to stop
      At every place:
   Up Stardust Hill,
      Down Rosebud Lane--
   Lamplighter, light
      The lamp again!

HAPPY LAND

MORE LITTLE PEOPLE OF LAMPLIGHT LANE

Happy Land

When you're asleep
 You travel far —
See, way out there
 Beyond a star,
Those steeples
 On that sleeping dot
Lie on a street
 You'd like a lot.

It REALLY **IS**
 A "different" town.
To say, "Hello" —
 you're upside down.

DOT LAND MAP

You say, "Goodbye"
 By lying FLAT.
This is NOT easy
 When you're fat.

The fire plugs
 Hang upside down;
A house burns UP
 It can't burn DOWN!

Few summer tourists
 Come to roam
Because this is
 The nesting home.
Of wobbly-wiggly
 Gyro-bats
And minny-binny
 Choc-lo-cats!

Gyro-Bats
And
Choc-Lo-Cats

The cats
 Are mainly
Fond of bats;
 And bats
Can gobble
 Scads of cats!

I don't see
 WHY
They MULTIPLY
 EXCEPT
 Their numbers
Run so High.

Wild Flying Bulls
  Are brave and strong—
Sails-in-the-wind,
   They bound along!

The Mouse-Nosed Lizard

These mouse-nosed lizards
    Puzzle us.
They'd even scare an octopus
    With stubby legs,
    With PILES of feet—
    It's very hard
    To keep them neat!

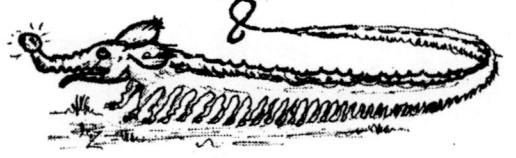

It takes a week
    To wash his toes
And clean his nails
    Before he goes
A slipper-slappin'
    Through the house—
That tidy-bidy
    little mouse!

A tomcat loves
    To run him races
Up banisters and
    And CREAKY places.

That cat would bat
Him in the gizzard,
BUT—
At quick escapes
Mouse is
A WIZARD!

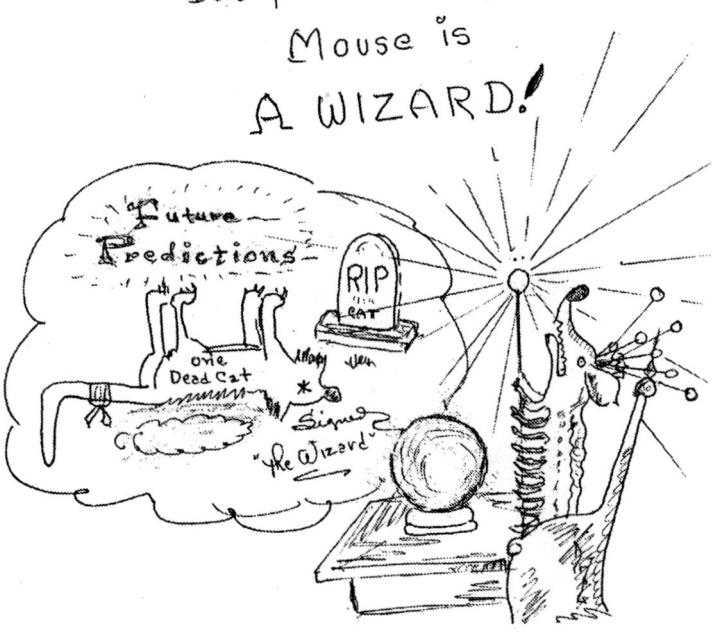

These ordinary
 Dinosaurs
Go Robbling 'round
 On two's
 And fours.

It's better when
 They fight and fuss
'Cause, otherwise,
 They'd gobble US.

```
        AND
        NOW—
       IF YOU
     WON'T CAUSE
       A FUSS,
    I'll BRING BACK
     IZZY AFTER US.
```
———

Question: He seems to travel very fast.
How long does his endurance last?
Answer: Not very long, I would suppose—
But longer than a rabbit's nose!

———

He will stop and sulk
  Down by the river—
He's a snobbish chap
And a non-forgiver.

Question: Well, do you think
  A child could pet him?
Answer: Never. He's cranky
  And bites if you let him!

———

Here's Izzyafterus again.
  Is he running from or for us?
Whichever way, it's safe to say
  He won't stay long and bore us.

The Cryworm

He hisses like a dragon,
  He travels like a snake,
And, though he looks so dangerous,
  This insect is a fake.

He will not bite at anything
  From beetlebugs to flies;
And when he spots a buttercup,
  He sighs, and sobs—and cries.

WILLIE, RUBE AND CHEE

By the blue water
In a cottage low and wee
   Lived three tiny fellows
Named Willie, Rube and Chee.

Willie was the worker
Baking cookies every day;
   Rube, sometimes, went fishing
But Chee played every way!

At last, Willie grew angry;
He cried at lazy Chee,
   "I'm hot and very tired--
Roll the cookie dough for me!"

"No, No-o-o-o-o, I won't!"
Called roly-poly Chee;
  "You come to the garden--
Play Ball and Jacks with me!"
  They argued; then they drew straws
Clutched tight in Reuben's paw
  To see for once and all
If work would be the law.

Willie As Artist

  The end of this tale
May surprise you in a way:
  "They're playing in the garden."
Well, that's what the tea leaves say!

Wink-a-Wunk

Well, here you have a Wink-a-Wunk
    Who looks like nothing but a "Clunk"
And if he thinks (though he seldom does)
    He only proves how dumb he was.

Once, a bumble bee bit hard.
    Well, he scratched his knee
Then he said, "I do THINK
    That's a FLY on me."

Now, he didn't raise his voice
    And he didn't turn his head,
Well, he barely blinked an eye--
    AND--
Then HE dropped DEAD!

A "Wundaby"

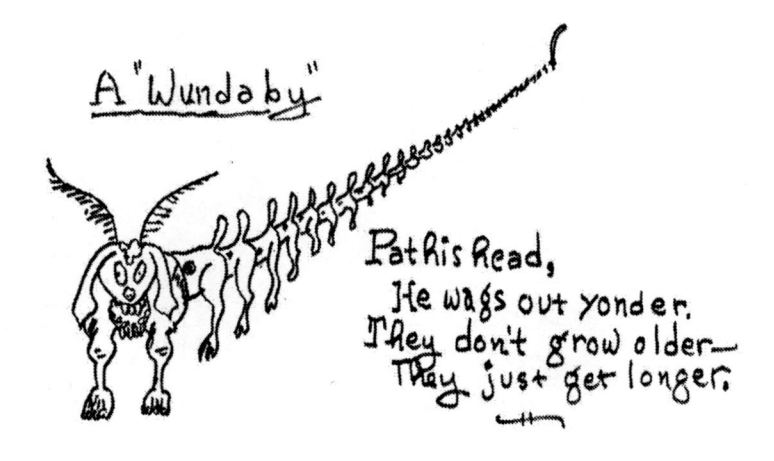

Pat his head,
  He wags out yonder.
They don't grow older—
  They just get longer.

Dearum's Snake

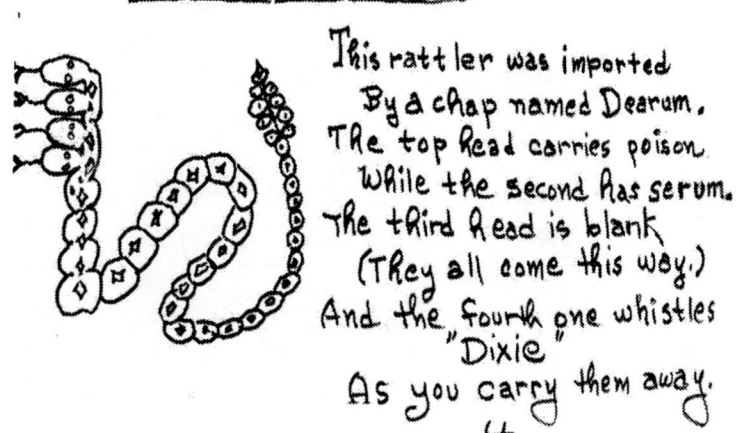

This rattler was imported
  By a chap named Dearum.
The top head carries poison.
  While the second has serum.
The third head is blank
  (They all come this way.)
And the fourth one whistles
  "Dixie"
As you carry them away.

His name is "Smorgie",
　If you ever saw him.
And, if you didn't,
　why DID you
　　Draw him?

Wunk-a-Wink

A Wink-a-Wunk and a Wunk-a-Wink
  Were walking by the creek.
Wunk yelled in wrath, "Go, take a bath!"
  Poor "Winkey" cried a week!
Then Wunk-a-Wink (How sad to say)
  Grabbed the soap and the towels
    And ran away —
  Just clowned and clapped
    And ran away.

Strange Bees

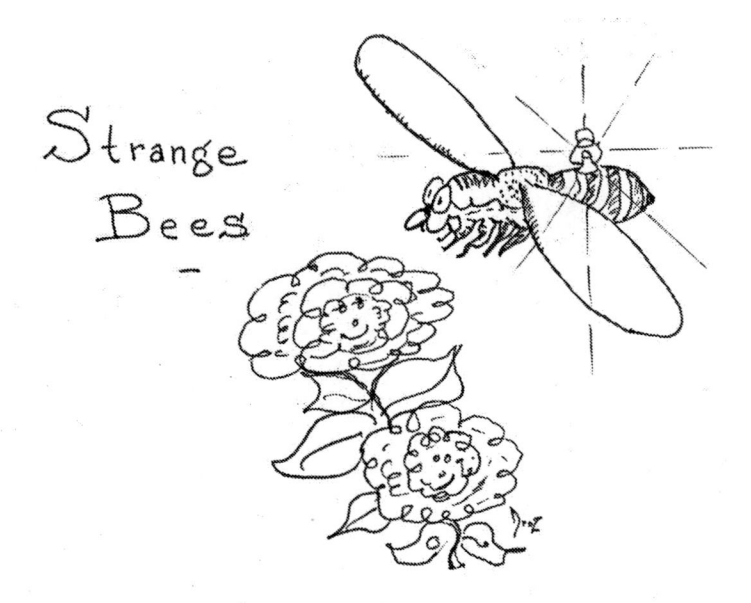

A lightning bug wooed
    And married a bee.
That was the strangest wedding
    you ever did see.

The children were peculiar —
    And ALL of them were odd —
Their wings looked much too big
    And their chests were very broad.

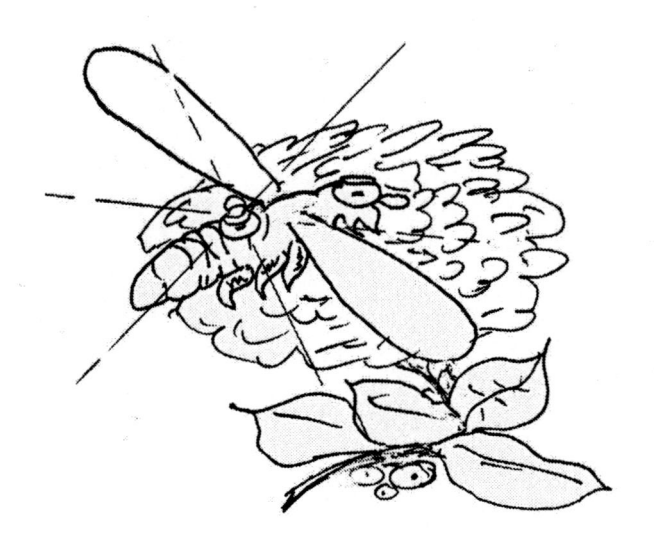

They worked long hours
    As <u>any</u> bees do
Gathering nectar
    The whole day through.

But, when shadows fell,
    Did they fly to the hive?
Not these strange bees—
    "Mercy Sakes Alive!"

They brushed aside moths—
    Even gave bats a fright,
Working all night long
    By lanternlight!

The tall lamplighter
　Now returning
Snuffs out the lamp
　So bravely burning,
And creatures of
　This nightly play
Slip past the curtain
　And steal away.

—

The shadows fold
　Their velvet wing,
And sleepy crickets
　Cease to sing.

—

The Piffawiffs with flying tails
　Go, scampering to the river dales
Where, vanishing with snorting fuss,
　Off gallops Izzyafterus.

—

The dew descends, but dreams will keep.
　Sweet children, rest in slumber deep:
The sun will rise and set — and then
　"Lamplighter, light the lamp again!"

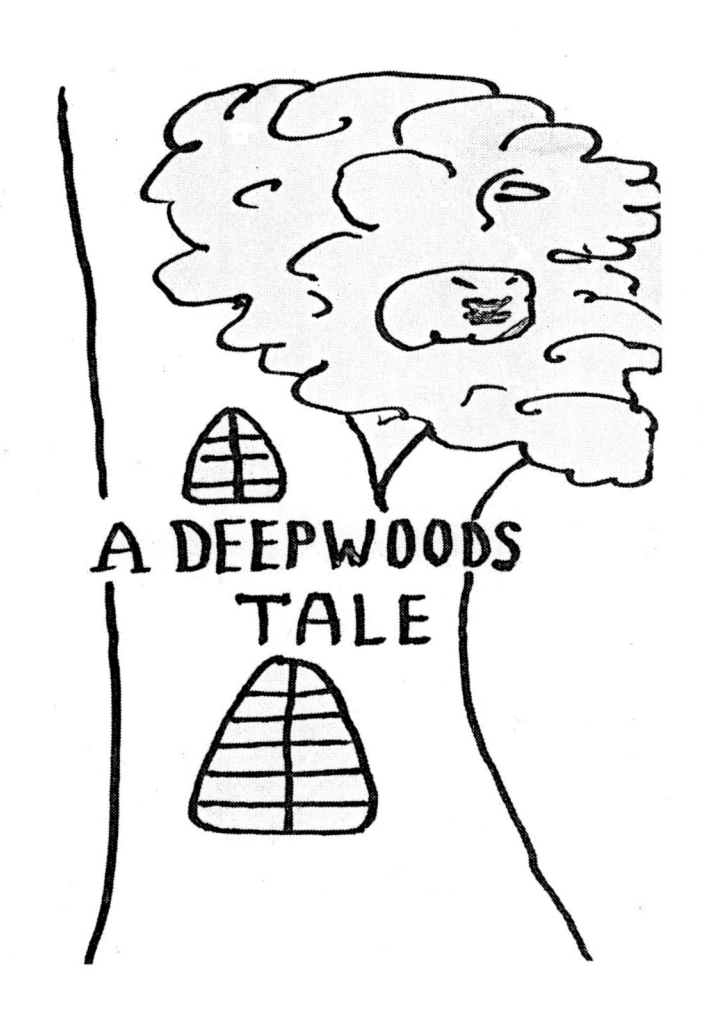

A DEEPWOODS TALE

A Deepwoods Tale

A possum, a coon, and an
    old black crow
Lived deep in an old
    hollow tree.

And the woods were deep;
    the woods were dark
        in groves that ran
            to the sea.

Well, Possum and Coon
        were both very fat,
           but Crow was
                skinny and wee.

One day he said, with a shake
    of his head,
"You two are a sight
    to see!"

Well, the possum got angry,
    and the coon had a fit;
And he cried, "Possum's fat—
    not me!"

What did Possum reply?
    "Coon's a pig—not I."
Then he heaved a big sigh
    deep down in the hollow tree.

"I will tell you this," said Coon.
"You're as silly as a loon
    to pretend that you're better
    than me.
The way you shovel in food
    is nasty and rude!
        That's disgusting—
           but you won't agree!"

"Well now," Possum said,
    with a toss of his head,
        "Who does eat the most?
        We will see!"

    Coon replied:
"I'll eat *nothing*—none at all
    till these clustered
        oak leaves fall.
    "I'll just wait and stay
        and stall
            in—this—tree!"

Possum shouted:
"Nor will I.
I won't budge here till I *die*!
I'll help watch
    the hours fly—
        patiently."

~ ~ ~

So, each went to his room
Locked deep in gloom.
    Only Crow
        left the hollow tree.
As he went out to shop...
    or perched at the treetop,
He thought,
    who'll the winner be?

But Possum won't budge,
And Coon can't nudge
    Tho the skin of 'is chin
        has shrunk!

They see food in their dreams;
Both are weary of schemes.
Each hopes his partner's unaware
    as each sad sap hits the *stair*.

Coon cries in a fright,
"If I don't eat tonight,
   in the morning
      I won't be there!"

~ ~ ~

It is dark as pitch
And as black as a witch,
   three A.M.
      in the Hollow Tree.
Possum opens the door,
No sound—not a snore;
   he is sure
      that the coon won't see.
Possum starts down the stair—
   "What is that?
      Who is there?"
         He trips, bumps and
            tumbles *down!*
BANG! BUMP! BOOM!
Clutching forms fill the gloom—
   "Burglars! Ghosts! Robbers are
      in town!"

Crow jumps out of bed
With a scarf around his head,
 in a tousled, tangled
  nightgown—
 with glasses askew,
 and so solemn, too,
  from the stairwell
   looking down.
What a vivid scene to view
Someone is pummeling who?

Old Crow strikes a light.
What a terrible fight!
"Hold up! Now stop!"
 he cries.

Possum nurses a cut lip,
Coon's tooth has a chip,
 and something's blackened
  both eyes!

Crow stands there in awe.
What a sordid scene he saw:
 They both look mini,
  very skinny
  and lean.

Their pants hang like bags;
    their clothes are in rags,
        plus they both look dirty
        and mean!

Possum looked at Crow.
And Crow ogled Possum.
    Soon
    they started to laugh!

Coon chuckled a bit.
Possum chortled a whit.
Finally crow whooped a
    howl-and-a-half!

    When
The fasting finally ended
    those folk were *never*
        quite the same.
Ole Possum stayed guanty.
While Crow was no-jaunty.
And how silly that quarrel
    became.

Yes, the laughter grew
    when the ruckus was through;
They yiped and rolled
    on the floor—
        and
Each one swore
    they'd fight—
        NEVERMORE!

~ ~ ~

"Come to the kitchen,"
    called Crow. "In a trice,
I'll whip up a porridge laced
    with chicken and rice."
He mixed it with curry,
    bacon stripped in a hurry;
Then the coon beamed at
    the possum—
        and he said,
            "That's nice!"

While all this was steaming,
With bright eyes gleaming,
Chef Crow checked the crocks
    and the bowls;

Then he stirred the beans
    with curry
And some bacon in a slurry
    steaming in a pot
        over coals.

• • •

    Let us pause for the moral:
      "It's so silly to quarrel
    whether coons, possums,
        or men.
    Because, when you start,
    you may break some heart
that can never be mended again."

• • •

Crow seized a spoon
    as he whistled a tune
        and tended the porridge
            with glee.
As soon as he was able
    he put the bowl on the table;
        Coon and Possum
            marched in to see.

With that big bowl
> between them,
>> I wish you could have
>>> seen them,
>> smacking their lips
> over tea.

First, the possum slipped
> the bread in—
Then the crow dipped his beak in,
> and Coon joined 'em
>> merrily.

They sopped, sipped, and supped,
> with no talk to interrupt;
>> and a crackling fire
>>> warmed the three.

And they still live together—
> good friends forever—
>> down in the Hollow Tree.

Old Dogs and Nature

THE BEGGAR'S SON

The lot of man is a rocky road,
    yearning to be wise and free.
Yet one weakness in some fellowmen
    is a lack of charity.

The beggar's son slept in the wood—
    having wandered full many a mile;
His feet were blistered by the stones,
    his face seamed with denial.

Raindrops spatter, as if in spite;
    the woods seem grim and dank.
A rosy sun disperses night
    as moonbeams ridge-ward sank.

A busy wren on neighboring boughs
    sang for the beggar's son;
He brook-ward hied to bathe and browse;
    his cloak's a tattered one;

Where do paupers find the will to live?
    whence comes hope to go on?
What prompts our hearts to pray and forgive
    on each primeval dawn?

Surviving thus, on faith and trust,
    as sunrise fills the glen;
Larks burst in song; we join along—
    now, wiser, happier men!

Note: Saved from a mouse-eaten scrap of paper in our barn, date unknown. I'm sure I wrote this bit for a "House By The Road" skit in the 1930s, originally read with musical accompaniment—Billy Phillips was our program adviser at radio KIDO Boise so long ago.

THE COMING STORM

A faint mist cloaks the sleeping wood
      where cloistered mosses fearful cling:
The drooping bough with veins unfill'd
      hangs lifeless, heeds no living thing.

Death marks the wren. The squirrel nods
      where gray owls droop their lagging wing:
Dark ghosts embalm the stony hills;
      deep, locked in earth, lie hosts of spring.

With ice-worn lips the huddling wind
      rattles along the broken stalks
Of tattered corn and ragged clods
      where gaunt crows taunt the vagrant fox.

The grumbling ocean chants a dirge
      more dismal than the seagull's call
As from the cold sleet breakers merge
      and, high o'erhead, with cloud-patched eye
The moon, a pirate, hurtles by
      until the black cloud smothers all!

IN THE CLAMOR OF A SHELL
(Motto: *A Little Beauty Is A Wondrous Thing*)

Did you ever marvel at a soft, pink petal
Or listen to the clamor of a shell—
      the whole world ringing in its orb of vastness?
If these things you have not done,
      O hear me well.

The ocean is a boundless, gliding fastness;
      O, to me a grain of sand seems vastly wide,
A tiny planet, crushed in shifting gambit,
      vies with wounded pangs—and mighty pride.

Did you ever listen to a soft-pitched strumming
      of dune-reeds shuddering in an ocean breeze?
Have you listened and perceived a deepened strumming
      of wind-tossed waves communing with the trees?

Take your eyes off the stars at morrow's borning;
      press your heart against the earth
           whence comes your breath;
You're only present for a fleeting hour—
      a pulse of Him who gains you back
           from Death!

Men are blind—some are deaf, or half demented.
      money! money!—pleasure! pleasure!
           Borrow! Lend!
Men throw away their God—
      a treasure they resented.
Surely knowing "Gold is vanquished
      in the end!"

Listen to a bird, earth's true muezzin',
      a soft-cloaked owl who wings the lonely night:
Like Isaiah, master of persuasion,
      owl *whoos*: "God is *all!* His greatness
          brings the world a light!"

Man is dust! Plain dust and cursed with clashes;
      hope, be infinite. Mercy, be our right!
Wild seas loft—sharp-toothed and ever whining—
      as ides conjure to lure our flimsy bark!

Time, a rat, gnaws at the world's broad stanchions;
      you'll hear him nibbling through the night
'Neath creaking sills with apt delight,
      as planets curve through cosmic tension;
Marauders, too, are men's invention.
We toss and suffer for our ills,
      propped by bandages and pills.

As a child you listened to Nature's chorus,
      peered at stars and galaxies a-blaze;
Tried to grasp at sintered clusters far above us;
      viewing the wheeling sky, a giant vase,
          filling it with missiles, helter-pace!

Buffaloes roamed hills, and pigeons, drilled
      on the veldts of ages—last;
Did the fond sun weep, butchered like sheep?
      Suddenly those "passerines" passed.
So the pigeons fell; buffaloes went to hell,
      prairie blow-flies had a blast!
O! Was it fair? Does anyone one care?
      only fools or poets ask—
          a meaningless task.

I decry the murder of those columns.
    my mind finds frozen words.
Random hoof beats burden my spirit,
    amid cries of dying birds!

I look aloft, the blue sky is naked;
    all quiet on Golgotha's hill.
Sounds of agony are silent.
    the field is bare, the bones lie still!
Not a passerine to kill—
    what an empty bill!

Thank God there are poets;
    praise God for good art!
Most men wear blinders,
    and have no heart.

Did you ever hearken to a sea shell sounding,
    thrust over an ear as when you were a child?
Why is that soft roar so enchanting—
    an enigmatic echo of the wild?

Have you stooped to hear a hiss
    sand grains are making?
Spied subtle colors of a blossom-bell
    dulcet-voicéd bees drone in a dell.
How can hunters kill creatures we love so well?

Look anew! Can your eyes frame the splendor
    of velvet skies at night—a cloud's array?
All aspects of our firmament are tender
    as barefoot boys skip gaily down-the-bay.

In age we change. Gone are the winging columns:
      red stains on guilty hands, in frozen curds;
Sounds of dying buffaloes vex my spirit;
      I hear revolting groans of dying birds!
          I'm short of words.

I look aloft, that blue-dome sky is naked;
      all's deathly quiet on Golgotha's hill,
The strife of souls in torture turning silent—
      this time, the killing fields are still!

Have you stopped to hear the sound sand grains are making;
      spy the halos that surround a blossom bell?
A dry weed rattles near a swaying primrose
      as dulce-voicéd-bees boot *bassos* through the dell;
         even drones like summer well.

Look—now! Your orbs are famed for splendor
      spying velvet skies at eve—a star's array.
All aspects of this firmament are tender,
      so sup their beauty *every* living day!

Note: Communism and the Berlin Wall capers were filling newspapers in 1963 when this poem was devised. Passenger or passerine pigeons of colorful hues flew in flocks that blotted the sun for days during their migration across America; all are gone now; one stuffed specimen resides in the Smithsonian I'm told. Buffaloes were wiped out as steam trains entered the scene. (Originally written 10 February 1963, Poulsbo, Washington.)

DEAD FOX SPEAKS

These groves are mine. And if I could,
    I'd say, *You're walking in my wood*;
And yet, I love to hear the sound
    of unknown feet on unknown ground.

The hermit thrush sings soft and clear,
    clematis trails the fence row near,
And starlight filters o'er this spot
    to comfort me, by men forgot.

The wending slug, he marks my grave
    and blunt moles blunder in my cave;
But it is lonely. And if I could,
    I'd say, *You're welcome in my wood.*

Note: In 1945, the Country Club Golf Course at Erland's Point had a narrow trail that begin only a hundred yards from our house. It skirted a woody tract where a hidden cabin stood on the slope above, completely hidden from view. This rustic log structure had been vacated by an original homesteader and was rotting away in an idyllic spot. An old drag-saw hung on a peg on the porch. A mossy barrel still stored rain, hard by the door. It was plain some person connected with the club had a weekend hide-away in this untouched bit of old memories. You could spot an ancient oil lamp on a rustic table just inside the window. Our children loved to search for wild strawberries, breathe the heady cedar-scented air and enjoy our secret trail. I thought of the wild creatures that once dwelt here, and I scribbled this poem under a fir, envying the chap who owned this redoubt. It is no doubt gone today, this November evening in 1997. These hideaways, like the dead fox , are ancient history now.

GLITTERING GOLD

It is written thus in the Scriptures: "Go to now, ye rich men, weep and howl for your miseries that shall come upon you. Your riches are corrupted, and your garments are moth-eaten. Your gold and silver is cankered; and the rust of them shall be a witness against you, and shall eat your flesh as it were fire."
---Chapter V, book of *James*

A kind saint, I am told, long years ago
    looked down from high Orion's vaporous cloud
And wept to see our sphere so wracked with woe.
    The Pleiades, perceiving, sobbed aloud
Or drew their twinkling lights from thirsty space
    to hide their tears who viewed the whirling ball,
Seeing idlers feast while kings and serfs disgrace
    God's handiwork with raucous bacchanal.

What could he think who viewed our maddened round
    of sinning stints and strife from dusk to dawn
As with listless handclaps we en-crown some sullen
    tyrant gorged with power and brawn?
Viewed he with tears alone? Nay! Far beyond
    mere human tears—he wept as Jesus wept
That men perceive not GOLD en-binds us all—
    it bids us bleed! Whence have we crept
From caverns and our clubs Neanderthal?

Note: Written for Radio, circa 1938. Revision, December 29, 1987.

THE KILLING FLOOR

Once, many years ago, Pauline and I boarded Amtrak in Seattle and debarked for Idaho. We detrained in Nampa to visit relatives, John and Nola Waite—and what a good visit. About then, Pauline's nephew drove in, and he said:

"You should visit Armour's Packing plant,
I work there—I'll guide ya through."
I did what all dumb tourists do.

Yellowed hand—written scribbles in a dusty box "somewhere," feature this surprising jaunt up old Armour's stairs. I pose no "moralics" as my memories thaw—just type up the notes—and here's what I saw:

"The Armour plant, at the edge of town, is small by most industry standards—killing and processing up to 300 carcasses in a shift—but its a productive plant, I don't think the equipment has changed much in umpteen years.

"We entered the plant from the back after being issued a hard hat—(important for protecting domes and chromosomes). Gregg's two tots accompanied me up a slope. (Those 'bitty' kids knew every rope with vision keen as a microscope.)

"We descended a long stairway and threaded to the 'dressing floor.' Halves-of-beef, hung on hooks thrust through a hind leg, readied for cold storage. The din was jarring! Workmen in company suits carried vicious tools. Huge knives swung on the belt of each' scout on the veldt of this carcass-conveyer-line!

"One man eviscerated the carcasses with deft passes of a power saw, cutting the cadaver from the throat down through the belly. Another worker pushed an ancient, cumbersome, three-wheeled cart with divided shelves, close to the animal, as entrails, liver and stomach juices rushed from its belly and gushed into various containers or compartments.

"After this was done, he wheeled the cart across the floor, dropping portions of the load, 'hither-and-non' to other conveyors. A fellow worker seized a 'juicy' liver, or whatever, and processed the item with gusto-robusto.

(Stomachs went another way; it was a tissue-roundelay.
Livers-and-bowels met back room scowls!
Please pardon the whimsy such crude subjects cause;
I need to relate 'em for that's how it was.)
There was a hefty odor, a smell of hides, flesh and sweat! Men worked rapidly and automatically; scrap heaps vanished quickly—nothing wasted.
Stomachs become 'tripe'.
While the wash of this 'stosh' was quickly annealing,
Smells welled—in the barrel—that were not appealing!

When Gregg applied the brake and opened the rig, he 'prosedly' said, printed big:
'It is a delicacy though it doesn't look it!
I tried to eat tripe once...and never again'.

"He had his wife bring me to the Armour plant. Gregg was running the stomach washer as we entered. The critter used vast quantities of hot water as food particles from a batch of stomachs revved in the barrel. The washer was taller than we were.

"At last, he braked the machine, removed the cover and showed us new-laundered stomachs, glowing pinkish–white; honey-combed chambers lined the inner sides.

"Gregg now conducted me (I was on crutches) and the two small boys, dwarfed by man-sized hard hats, into the fore part of the killing floor.

"From our vantage point, we watched eight or ten workers threading constantly in and about the slow-moving line of carcasses. Ahead of the man who eviscerated carcasses was the hide-puller who fastened a chain—clamped it to the hide, at the root of the tail—and inexorably pulled the hide off.

"Ahead of him was the electric shock unit where the beef 'cadaver', still uncut, hanging by a hooked-leg, swung around the curve on a steel rail and stopped, dead, still before a compartment that read:

> **DANGER, HIGH VOLTAGE!**

"At this juncture, a curved pipe, formed in a 'U', was thrust against the belly of the carcass. A charge of electricity was applied. It rose and fell in rhythmic jerks that lessened (but lingered) until all nerves and muscles ceased to respond. Out it came; a new one took its place, a steady stream.

> The cadavers jerked eerily for a lengthy heat—
> Such acts relax taut muscles and tenderize the meat;
> So Hi! Ho! To-Mall we go,
> In racked-cuts for a Deli,
> To feed the brutes in city suits and curly headed Nelly!"

(I must admit there were no Malls or Deli's at the time my notes were written, but I can't resist a little 'twist', by funsome-punsom's bitten.)

"Gregg ushered me and the two small boys to the front of the killing line, loaded with carcasses, freshly killed and still quivering. Two men on a platform, eight or ten feet above us, were busily cutting off heads and hooves:

Water, blood and spatters of both pulse above us.
Multiple droplets continue to shower our forces—
'baptismal remorses' from freshly-killed corpses.
This is, I imagine, what a 'charnel house' would be.
Men must work-the-beat so their kids can eat.
It would spell defeat for me!

"The workers, for the most part, though grimly busy—would smile as they caught our eye. Perhaps they found humor in the unscheduled appearance of an aging man on crutches and two small boys with yellow hard hats dipping over their eyes. The boys, by the way, had been here before and 'just could hardly wait' to see the scene again. A child of three and one of five seemed to revel in discussing this 'magic' scene. They talked about seeing the guts ripped out of the cattle—making references to gory scenes-again and again—getting in as close as possible, to watch and get entangled, I decided.

"As we threaded between a tangle of hanging beef suspended by a single hook attached to one ankle of their huge legs, I envisioned how easily we could be crushed if an animal broke loose. This was by far the most dangerous-and-vulnerable point for onlookers or workers in the plant; we were near the front of the killing floor.

"The man in the pit caught my eye; he was in the most vulnerable place of all. Two beef animals had just been killed and a huge door revolved by a lever trigger and, I suppose, hydraulic power—tumbled them over on the floor where he stood. They were kicking violently. His job was to secure a chain to a hind leg at the ankle and raise them aloft by electric winch. I was told he had once been struck by a kicking beef that had broken both his knees. Another version was, he had a long stint in the hospital with two broken knees from a kicking animal, or by one falling on him that broke loose from the chain. I'm not sure which is right. These animals appear to be dead; but their reflexes still respond; they are dangerous and unpredictable, in any case.

"I dipped between two steel posts and climbed a short stair, relieved that we had seen what I supposed was the worst of this grotesque 'ballet'. That was a mistake indeed! Suddenly, the two little boys and I were sandwiched in a cubicle while cattle moved through all this mayhem, on their own power—and for what? The answer was apparent; mass execution was their final award!

"The defile was narrow enough that only one animal could stand in this chute. The fear was evident in each quivering beast, as they were prodded into position. Gregg took a small gun-like object two or three inches in diameter and about ten inches long. In one end of this he placed a charge smaller than a thimble, secured it and aimed it above the head of he nearest beast. There was a loud pop and the animal fell, immediately threshing in its narrow cell.

"The beast behind it, eyes filled with terror, tried to escape but eventually fell, victim to the same adroitly placed charge. It was over.

"Someone must do it, I know, but I'm not made of stuff stern as this.

"The two small boys leaned over the rail, getting close as possible, with wonder and awe in their eyes, but they were not shocked as I was. All they appeared to feel was excitement or even exhilaration.

"This 'blood and gore' was heady stuff—I am continually amazed at children—one cannot predict their responses at any age. I decided we would enjoy our exit.

"Armour expects to close the plant in about two

weeks. Union wages here are running too high, they decided. When the plant reopens it will be non-union, and they say beginning pay will be around $5.00 per hour, at that time in 1984.

"I would not want any part of that plant at any price. There is much danger here, more than I recall seeing in any other places except, perhaps, rock crushers, mines, rigging sites and sawmills. (You can name more, I am sure.)"

Gregg is a good looking, stalwart young man. He would not have chosen this work except for the wages and fringe benefits it provided.

"Some men worked in this plant over thirty years—thirty 'eons' of noise, smells, confusion, discomfort, ever-present danger and constantly-moving effort—and (I am sure) boredom.

"Now, their jobs come to an end! What will they do, I ask you! Draw compensation—or live in Poverty's Shoe, traditionally blue?"

Gregg's brother, Danny, moved here from the Midwest a couple years ago. Danny has a well-established security business in nearby Boise. Gregg plans to go into partnership with Dan and establish a security branch in Nampa. I wish them well. As for you who read this history 'fiss', a bonnie farewell!

FINIS

This material was salvaged from the sheets of a pastel, charcoal and crayon newsprint paper tablet I often carried on vacation jaunts. There were no pictures this time, just scribbles. I spent hours deciphering the hasty thoughts I jotted on the site—and in the evening of that doleful day. Armour's is not an ideal subject but the facts are here to stay. The little boys were truly there and loved the entire day!

THE RATIONEERS

From 1942 to 2001 is quite a step. Let's try to recapture a World War II memoir: The Japanese had bludgeoned us so adroitly, we were truly fearful of further attacks (especially on the West Coast). I was working for the Personnel Office of Shop 51, at the Puget Sound Naval Shipyard. Shop 51 was called the Electric Shop. One of my duties was handling rationing problems for the entire shop's crew.

On a daily basis, I took the worker's applications for rationing directly to the Gas Rationing Office in an ancient-and-classic building, yanked from prestigious moorings and plumped down near the waterfront. I loved that daily jaunt, *via* shank's mare. That duty often took two to three hours of my time.

Much of my day was spent in filling out worker's requests for gasoline, shoes, or what-have-you. There was a large book at that office that was a bulwark for Ration Board Dignitaries; the staff of that office took their jobs very seriously.

There was a very attractive Navy Wave in the Ration Board Office. One day I complained to her about a decision the board had made. One of our electricians had been denied the proper amount of gasoline. That was my opinion of the matter, anyway. Perhaps I was a bit loud about it. The lady officer ordered me to vamoose! So I did.

Next day, I wrote the following poem and politely handed it to her. From that day on we were mutually respectful. But I do believe, afterward, we got better treatment in Shop 51. The power-o'-the-pen.

TO O.P.A. (Apology)

Deep in file-cluttered dens there sit,
Well-fortified by cigars and wit,
(And spectacles that "mirror justice"),
These hallowed gents who never trust us.
These spiders spin a web of rations
In paradoxic "O.P.Ations."
How they connive to weave devices
Of "ipso facto's" and in such wise's--
Incomprehensive? Their public prankdom
Is dreamed up in this noble sanctum
That ties poor yokels up in knots
Like sinners in the devil's pots.

Don't scream or moan, O helpless mortal!
But beg your bread while members chortle
Knee deep in B's and C's and rations
(Perhaps piled up for debtor nations).
Behind these hallowed doors, when seen,
The "brass Hat" goes with humbled mien;
And even he who wears the chevron
Must stoop to ask, by grace of Heaven,
Might he be issued for stated uses
Those humbly needed petrol-juices?

Swear not! <u>Speak not loud</u> in this abode
Where even saints have penance strode,
But mind thy lip and guileful look
Lest they remove thy ration book!
O! Stir ye not the wrath of gods,
Or, gasless, shalt thou trod the clods.

So, dear Lord, give us strength of seven
(And all the wit and tact in heaven!)
That we escape the biting sword
They wield there in the Ration Board!

And may you full with grace endow us,
So we're respectful when they cowe us--
To question not the root of evil
But give his due to saint or devil!

Yea, Lord, we ask that in the future
No caustic rule, nor word, nor suture
Shall stir our calm, warm smile, O Lord,
When we greet that "sweet, dear" Ration Board.

COLLYWOBBLE REQUIEM

Up a collywabble canyon, climb the rill
Sweet Dolly May; then skether through heather
In the "Meadows of Jollay"—I hope you light—
I s'pose you might on such a lovely day!
(A gypsy chap in feathered cap is hollerin' "*Olay!*"

When there's frostin' on the medders
And bills singe your toupee
Don't holler like a "brawler,"
Shet yer shoes and sneak away—
(Here, livin's loose an' breezy;
So, just toss them bills away!)

Th' meads-and-weeds of Collywobble
Are where boosters come to play,
Silly cherubs in their bare-hubs,
Toss their boots and feel passé.
There's no ticket to this play!

Diamond picks slay ukuleles
And the snow's as warm as milk.
Cherubs never thief-a-kerchief
If it *'tisn't-raided-silk*—
And the jokes they tell aren't funny
If your "Scotchy" with the money!

Come and dance—sweet baby-hunny,
In them funny, bunny 'scants.
I wear sneakers when it's cooler
(Like some 'la-de-dah' preschooler),
But I wouldn't be a fool—er,
Play the clown in fancy-rants!

"R" is for "realistic"
When yer old and statistic,
For ya know your days are numbered
And the wolf who tracks ya scowls—
If mater's domineering and the Ides-O-Woe
Are leering, just yell "Hi De Ho!"

Fast gearing—and don't fear the wolves and owls.
If my poem be-tomes-me-silly
And you're a haughty *filly*.
I'm just jokin', I ain't broken,
Writin' muh poetric-quillry.
Cause my folks they all were "Switzers,"
Not a bunch of idle snitzers!
We didn't come from France
Or wear frilly Holland pants.

Finale Operastale

Come to Collywobble Canyon.
"Nappy" never had a chance
To be Happy. What a sap he,
On that island where he rants!
So, anon, dear tiring reader;
I have courage, here to say,
"It ain't schmoolish to be foolish.
So long. Have a fruitful day."

LINES TO AN OLD BROWN DOG

I shall always revere the memory of this understanding friend and companion. His knowledge of nature was a moving revelation. More than ordinary companions, we felt a kinship beyond words. Though he often slept on an open porch, he did not seem to mind when icicles gathered on his shaggy winter fur.

His throaty bark sounded through the night when danger was nigh, supposed or real. His intention was to guard and obey. How well he understood our needs.

His intelligence, good will, and happy outlook were continually reflected in those expressive, brown eyes—an aristocrat clothed in the shabby garb of a cur. A true example of the range in God's handiwork, a paradox of humble ignorance and aristocracy—a beggar, yet a saint who wolfed our table-scraps as if gathering manna from heaven.

A kind word was his fee, plus the reward of a smile and a stroke of our friendly hands. In age, he was still a child; in youth, he was wise with inborn knowledge some dogs possess. He knew what the wind said of weather. He felt the surge of spring when first blades of green crouched beneath the winter thistle.

Here is my tribute to a departed teacher, scholar and friend to whom I owe the debt of countless happy hours undimmed by harsh words or misunderstandings that have marred so many human friendships. Lines to a brown cur, a spark of something far more grand than mere pedigrees produce. He knew his place. Limitations were evident. But he was fortified with intuitive instinct.

In short, he was a faithful, loving, disreputable old dog who lived and died true to creeds and dictates of his forbears:

How often, as a pup, I watched him play
    where hedges press against a garden's edge—
Or, joyful, heard his glad bark greet the day
    as gaily as a blackbird in the sedge.

And, oft, in winter, bathed in driving sleet
    that from some black cloud fed a dreary night,
Upon the weathered stoop he aimed his feet
    in calm obeisance curled in fading light.

Serving us through years of patient due, content with
    table scraps, head-pats or scanty play,
Cow-towing to our needs, the peevish whims
    that selfish boys enlist on idle days.

"Come Buster! Fetch the cows! Here Buster, play!"
    Next day: "Doggy, go home—vamoose, I say!
Don't tag, old fag—for Pete's Sake, Just go-way!"

How often, on the drab-brown earth espied,
    I watched him wile the eager hours away
Digging for a mole where earth was pried,
    poising to snatch some field mice in the hay.

Can better praise of him than this be said
    of a faithful friend entangled in our toil:
Who never by the fire could rest his head;
    he served his masters well; he loved the soil.

He was a patient listener, warm and wise,
    and paid us lavish tribute with his eyes.
Where often as a pup I watched him play;
    only a wooden stake defines his bones today.

His name's on a scroll in a roll-top desk log.
How can I e'er forget that "chowsy," bow-wowsy,
    happy old dog?

Note: Written for the radio in the late 1930s.

THE POPLARS

The poplars glow beyond our wall,
    they toss like ships upon the sea,
And they are staunch, so very tall,
    as tall as any church should be—
But I am very small!

Now, if there were no poplars here,
    I doubt that I would care to be!
The poplars love to brush at me;
    they whisper messages of cheer.

They have good reasons here I know—
    their boughs I bend with Indian glee;
To make a bow, aloft I go
    and cut a stout, green limb and see
The blue canal and men that mow.

Then, I forget my Indian ways
    and wonder if the poplar tree,
Perhaps, grew up so tall and sways
    to get a better view of me
On lazy, golden Autumn days.

Note: This reminisce stems from Robert Louis Stevenson. Many of his poems celebrated childhood visions, as in 'Land Of Counterpane'. I too, was bedfast for a long time on the Cotterel desert. There were no trees at that period. My love for poplars stems from that episode. We had a long lane of Poplars at Declo, our next venture after Cotterel.

HILL DAISIES

Pale stars lie agleam in the grass
Warmed by touch of springs that pass,
Although the lilac bud is hardly green
And dead vines from off the trellis lean.

I walked upon a rocky hill, alone,
Marveling how little grew in barren stone,
When, suddenly, my heart a gladness knew;
For there, moist and fragile, blown with dew,
Some shy little flowers beamed at me.

Like the pale fingers of a star
Shining through mist and battle scar,
Each one alight! It seemed my feeble thought
Bore out no blessed beauty that it ought
On seeing such a miracle in space,
So small they seemed—so little sod they graced.

Their tender petals, enigmas of birth,
Were spying on the sun in happy mirth;
And suddenly new warmth and joy I knew
Because on that bleak hill the daisies grew.

Note found at the bottom of original poem: The sun creeps up higher toward the zenith, slowly the pound and throb of the city beneath breaks into your reverie—you hear the hollow boom of the switch engines as they break and connect long strings of cars on glittering lanes of steel. You descend to the world of paved walks and noisy strife, but the light is still with you, for you know that on a barren bluff a wild scented April wind is rustling the petals of a cluster of fragile white flowers imbedded in the red sandstone.

SOMETHING SEPTEMBER

There's something in September—
    an almanacal spread.
"Take care! *Dad-Fall* is coming,
    and winter storms we dread!"

Bright sunshine, in September,
    imparts a rosy glow,
And trees, in dappled-orchards,
    with fruit are bending low.

The wild geese are now veeing
    in platoons overhead.
Buckbrush on the mountain
    is donned in robes of red!

Bold autumn is a season
    When fat sheaves fill their krall
As golden pumkins glisten;
    O, yes! I love it all!

EARTH AND HEAVEN

New, every river ever seen
    to sweep its tidal bay
Is like a bit of melody,
    the rippling water's lay
Holds echoes of the mountain brook
    in the hollow of its hand
The roar of tempests that have shook
    the forest's Titan strands,
The echo of the woodland dove
    that sighs among the boughs,
The singing of the meadow breeze
    where lowing cattle browse,
And the sweetest serenade of all,
    where larks o'erwing the mead
The rhyming chant of springs that fall
    and over granite speed—
A song that does outpour the life
    of every tiny seed.

It holds the rain unto its breast;
    the pure gleam of the snow
Does break upon its paneled crest;
    and burnished with its glow
The stars give it a million eyes
    where casual brooding moonlight lies
In close cropped thickets 'lorn of shoot,
    it hastes to lave the thirsty root.
It shuns not nettles spiny green
    nor holds shrub or leaf too mean
To share the enervating flood
    which is their very life and blood.

Where fleeting hares have sought retreat,
    the roses lift their willing lips,
The prim deer sips its beverage sweet
    where close the crannied springlet drips:
The herbage lies in secret flower
    along the aspen shaded bower
Where rudely the kingfisher cries
    and liquid songs of blackbirds rise
Enraptured where the starbeams play
    in that clear crystal of its bay
Upon the heavens *mannaed* plain
    above high columns bowed with grain
And green lush seas with grassy spires
    where stars o'er hang
        their close-lamped fires
Above a cerulean sea
    may some sweet singing river be.

Our solace and our grace up there—
    a holier and purer stream
Than ever down these hillsides gleam.
May they upon that height discern
    where bright those starry tapers burn
A river winds its gallant thread
    whose echoes wake the silent dead
And beat upon the tranquil air
    in throbbing echo like a prayer.

The Midnight Poet

THE MIDNIGHT POET

The poet got up in the mid-of-the-night
And dug for a tablet in frenzy to write.
No notice he paid to his nightcap askew
Or how bold the wind through his cold attic blew.

His slippers are barely attached to his feet,
As he dons rough, old trousers a-bag in the seat.
A guttering candle he sticks to the table—
And writes just as fast as his fingers are able.

Down pour ideas; with gusto he lines' em,
Chews on a pencil—removes or refines 'em.
No notice he takes as the night hours fly,
Rewriting foolscraps with frowns and a sigh.

He scratches the old pate, now nearly uprooted,
Like a lad on a date whose improperly suited.
At work he's berserk, forget all the wrinkles—
The serious eyes harbor nary-one twinkle.

Well could he be E. Poe in the offing,
Or Dryden, imbibin' some critical scoffing,
Old Wordsworth, a Shelley, Lord Byron or Keats:
But, due age, his sad Muses sit—glued in their seats.

Though Brontes, like Satyrs, cavort in his room,
He hides, like a mummy, in trappings of gloom.
How scanty's this mode; he's desperately smitten,
Like 'kinder-G-kittens' who lost all their mittens!

Scant rhythms ride with'im, this myopic scholar,
A scrivening old saint with seldom a dollar.

And yet, to the world may history endear him,
If greatness and wisdom despair coming near 'im;
T'would be too unjust should the world just ignore,
Or by too-grim truth, announce him a bore.

He's poor and so bumbly, but his soul is a giant—
A chore-man of woe, his memory is pliant.
Who knows, deep within him a pyre is burning,
Though, from his pen, flows only scanty discerning.

His is the role few mortals will master!
Be you great, be ye small, fell Time is the tasker
Who limits our lives to puny successes
While sod o'er the graves of our 'noblest' she presses.

Strive on, quaint scribe, though chastened by Time,
Good purpose surpasses the fault of your rhyme!
And those who shed laughter upon this poor knave,
May yet lay a wreath and a tear on his grave.

A TEASDALE SEA

A simple girl, unwed—alone
Lives in a manse of 'noble stone'.
Rich parents watch; few kin to spare,
Lonely poets are everywhere.

She wrote: "I never saw a moor;
I never saw the sea;
Yet I know how heather looks
And what a wave must be."
Visions flowed smoothly from her pen,
Here, at my window, cold tides "Amen!"

Peering through an attic pane,
Old Puget glides with drumming rain.
Each time I ride the ferry,
Watch seagulls "tour the flow,"
I try to match sweet Sara's glow;
(I'm a poetry buff—you know.)

"Tigers raging through elephant kraals!"
Excite boy readers in overalls—
Like Kipling, who wowed the Brit's parlay
With spanking tales of Mandelay.

I marvel that Emily seemed to know
Of ocean storms and flying spray:
Her lines out-mime my rhyme's array
Although 'her ocean' was far away!

A MAIDEN LIES DREAMING

Beside the calm river a maiden
    lies dreaming,
Though marble has hemmed her
    upon every side.
She sleeps in the stillness of
    bright bowers gleaming,
By a beautiful river that rolls
    to the tide.

As pure was her beauty
    as roses red-glowing
O'erfilled with the richness of
    meadows and dew,
As I, in the springtime
    of beauty's going,
Swore nothing could sever
    the bliss that we knew.

Maiden of reverie, come to me
    in dreaming
As once when I held you
    so close in my arms.
Alas, there's no power brings you
    to my dreaming,
And nothing awakens your
    sweetness and charms.

Then, rest you, my darling! In bright
    bowers gleaming,
Though marble has hemmed you
    upon every side,
And rest you, my love, as forever
    in dreaming
You sleep by the river that rolls
    to the tide.

THE SKELETONS

(Written on the steps of the U.S. Post Office, Seattle,
Washington, 15 June 1942.)

Upon the storied marbles nigh,
I stood while skeletons marched by.
The puppets passed in promenade
In rags, and gold, and jewels arrayed.
With steps that spring, the youth goes here
As old age marches up with fear
In every step. In harbored lee
The Ships are resting, fresh from sea:
I wonder why the peaceful sky
Makes mankind's vaunted peace a lie!

We bow we smile, we nod we laugh;
We grow impatient as we quaff
The liquors of our glutted brewing
And make our life our life's undoing.
I ask, old friend, why—all the while—
Sad mourners weep as bridegrooms smile;
And youths, impetuous, laugh and lie
On beds of love while thousands die?
The boiling pot of greed and class,
The city has a heart of brass.

These all are but a foot from death!
An inch, a sigh, a tear, a breath
But separates them from the clod—
The fearful silence that is God:
Less clowns and actors than but frail
And foolish beasts, our great travail
Is to fill our bellies—to propagate—
To sate the sense, and cry too late.

Men speak of love. The muted word
Dies on the lips that scarcely stirred.
And so, beside these columns,
I stand watching skeletons go by
Upon the endless belt of street,
Marching to death on hurrying feet.
Laughing, bowing, being contrite,
Acting courteous and polite,
Cursing, cowering and struggling on
Go the fawning cripple—the pompous don,
The militarist with starchy braid.
All staring at death, and undismayed.

When I think of the numberless, lonely ways
All gathered so close in the book of our days,
I think that words are a poor, cheap lie
When, in spite of customs, I wonder why
All men must marry, worry and strive
And almost beg to stay alive!
Though none will admit but the sorriest few,
We all are beggars, if we but knew,
Who beg for the crust of a hidden joy
As we weep for the love that our lusts destroy.

By these stately pillars, poised and high,
The skeletons are marching by.

THE TWO BLIND MEN

I.

He stood aloof in all the throng.
What did he think? No one could say;
His sightless eyes were dull as coal,
No light reflected from his soul,
And grief had drained away.

Mutely, listlessly he stood
Like a lonely monk in a mourner's cloak;
The look upon his face was wood—
And no one stopped—and no one spoke.

An echo's distance down the street
Another waif in selfsame guise,
Like a leper haunting paradise,
Annoyed the casual passerby,
By standing there with sightless eye
In sad obeisance of his clan
Which men ascribe a blinded man.

Near each one there was a sign,
Beside each man a pencil stack,
And on each face a look that bore
An image of the mental wrack
Misfortune brings as heretofore:
And yet—a difference was plain.

They looked alike in broadest sense:
Both menial, worn; both frayed and bent
And crushed by fate's impenitence;
Still, one man lived, though one was spent.

II.

Upon the first man's chest there was
The usual sign that does remind
A passerby who hurries past:
So many men are blind!

Ah! What a difference there would be
If living did not press so much,
If gifts and love were really free,
If gold were really good to touch.

III.

Some men walked near him—some walked far
Around him. With passive air,
He turned his lean face toward the sky
As though there was no other there—
As if he did not care.

A sign, too, hung upon his coat,
Beside him, too, a pencil stack
That no one seemed to touch at all!
Yet, all around him, front and back,
The gleaming dimes and coppers fall—
And there is something queer in that!

You would have seen, had you walked by,
That something quickened every eye
That could be quickened when they saw
The simple placard that he wore,
A sight they'd never seen before.

And what a difference there would be
If lips could utter no deceit,
If all who hungered could have meat—
And yearning eyes could see!

IV.

The first man's life *was* drowsy night;
The other still remembered day.
Dear God! Let no one dim the light
That is his soul—that lets him pray
To see a star again some-day
And helps him dare the night;

For he who strives to brave the dark
While other men are seeing
Needs more than coins to feed a spark
That warms our weary being.

The Easter time had come and gone,
The winter fogs were cleared away;
And even in the city air
One caught the scent of lilac spray.

A blind man sat upon the street
As other blind men hurried by
But theirs was blindness of the soul—
And his was but the eye.

Many who went hurrying by
Turned back to drop a dime;
And many heaved a pensive sigh,
While others had a moistened eye—
And then, of course, some idlers yawned.

I cannot tell you how
He did this miracle—I say,
A miracle it was that day;
But here is what he wrote
That caught in many a throat,
That made the laborer pause in the street,

And the financier look down
With a puzzled frown.
It was not cutting; it wasn't unkind;
Just: *"It is May, and I Am Blind."*

Note: Written in 1948, based on an article in *Coronet Magazine* of that year, perhaps the May 1948 issue. Dwight R. Droz, Scandia Patch Press.

FANCY'S BURIAL

Gone are my days serene,
    gone is my youthful light.
And my heart sleeps fitful in a casket of flesh—
    my soul strives day-and-night!

The owl, who hoots in his covert,
    he chides my weary sleep,
I wish I could bury fancy here,
    to bury him deep—ah, deep!

The critical eye of the heartless, nigh,
    the lips that rebuke and frown;
These, too, shall wither bye-and-bye,
    and the green earth mold 'em 'round!

All words that buttered my tongue with speech
    have grown so wearing and trite
That should I lie where gay blooms peep,
    or were I pressed in the sod;
Scant need to weep of "Deathly-sleep,"
    so near *am* I to God!

A LAMENT

The fire turns to ashes;
   the brook no longer sings.
And all the heart remembers
   seems old, forgotten things.

The lad who roamed the meadow,
   the mare who tensed the plow
Are dead as "old tomorrow"
   and no one needs them now....

My garden grows untended;
   a wine-press rusts 'neath the vine.
Now glowing years have faded—
   down fallen and supine.

The aspen and the willow
   that cloaked a host of song
Seem wan, withdrawn and yellowed,
   trembling leaves will soon be gone.

The colt who tagged the furrow,
   a mother who tensed at the plow,
Are dead as beards on the bureau;
   no one remembers them now.

A smithy's hearth is seldom seen;
   the anvil hardly rings:
A carriage on the village green
   might seem a gruesome thing.
I hear once more the droning bees,
   the charm of chanting rills,
While cricket's sonant revelries
   encase the purple hills.

With nighthawks o'erhead flowing,
    the cattle trapped in-shed
Set up a plaintive lowing,
    impatient to be fed.

The sorrel team with tugs up-tied
    marches wearily down the lane;
Apple blossoms fume far and wide;
    the breeze bares hints of rain.

Huge poplars raise their gusty arms
    to quaff a honeyed breeze.
The sparrows posit mild alarms
    and quarrel in the trees.

A meadowlark, her wings outspread,
    rollicks o'er wind blown rye:
How can you forget the sonnet she sings
    under a summer sky?
Our lives are strings of such wonderful things;
    these moments should never die!

Note: From a sheet found, an un-finished scrap.

SAMMY THE CROW

"That crow is back!" Pauline said, pulling the covers off me.

"You mean just a couple, don't you?" I said when I came awake. "Sammy and Louie."

"Well, yes, there are two coming up on the corn patch by the road."

I grabbed up the sixteen gauge and started for the front door. There wasn't a crow in sight. They'd read my mind. For several mornings I tried to get a clear shot. I couldn't shoot toward the neighbor's house or where cattle stand near the fence. Those two clever crows picked an angle where some farm animal is in the way; if the coast seems clear but no bovines are near, they wing on, those elusive devils!

I looked out the window. A darn crow stood right there in the garden—right where I didn't dare fire on him—might hit a neighbor's house or a car driving by. Flivvers really zip down Scandia hill when you least expect them.

While there were only two birds, one of them was most brazen. I managed a long range snap at him one week ago and missed, as usual. I aimed carefully, raised the barrel a mite for distance—but no help. I nicked him two years ago; he just flew away cussing every flap.

Last year I went through one-and-a-half boxes of shells over a two-week period. The sage birds finally decided they'd had sufficient fun.

They enjoyed my geriatric tricks; I'm sure. But posing to entice me at a very long range soon bored them. Perhaps they even conjectured the odds for a bull's-eye improved with each fusillade of my Sears and Roebuck shotgun.

They deserted the field and moved down the line for a time. Then, to prove they weren't cowards at all—they looted our cherry trees, ca-a-wing with every gulp.

"Come on, fellows," gritty voices rang. "Sweet cherries! Sweet cherries! Six-thirty-three northwest Scandia road!"

They melted away when I came running. The only cherries we picked were those they dropped; the trees were wholly bare. They won!

I neglected to mention how they read our minds. I've heard it said crows may count some place below ten. If five people walk into a blind, and four come out, the crow says to himself, "H'm—m-m, let me see; four guys came out, but five went in. A'ha, there's still one guy waitin' in there, poor fool him!"

Then he raises a beak, rocks in a peculiar manner and cries "Ca-a-a-a-aw! Ca-a-a-aw!" To himself, he mutters, "What chumps those humans are!"...and exits laughing.

Encyclopedias claim crows can live up to seventy five years, so there's a lot of know-how stored in that smart, black head; the eye is bright, keen and perceiving.

And this was the ritual. Sometimes they would stand way off and beg me to shoot, to liven dull times, or they'd soar overhead with loud, bragging cries to let their buddies know I'd missed.

So this morning I took a new tactic and put the shotgun at ready on the tractor seat. Said I, "We'll fool those tittering-thugs."

In the past they cast a clear-cut rule. People driving tractors have both hands full, they do not shoot when whooping-it-up—bouncing over potholes in third gear. Now, if a farmer stops the rig, it's time crows depart. This is a well-known rule of the art. In the case of farmer Droz, if he aims he'll miss—any buzzard on the slope could tell you this (he misses more than nine times out of ten).

Sammy and Louie depart, only to alight in a tree in a neighbor's pasture and stare brazenly.

"You know, Louie," Sammy says, "I think ol' man Droz's eyes are getting' worse."

"Well," Louie replies, "he hasn't been real steady since that fateful trip when he come back from Mayo's 'surge-a-ree' with a steel rod in his hip."

"Yeah," Sammy proclaims. "If a new farmer came with better aim, *then* we'd wish we were still stuck with this old sinner."

With a flap they saunter off to Pearson Point beach to latch a clam dinner.

That afternoon, with the gun at the house, they come back for a closer gander. They figure, no doubt, I've left the double barrel home: both are sassy and full of dander, following down the furrows zapping worms as the diesel purrs.

I enjoy their capers that the long afternoon.

They know I don't have the shotgun; it makes them careless.

Says I, "Those crows will soon bug off; they don't hang around much past five. They have a communal perching grove. They won't come back tonight." I don't say this out loud, that's how your mind works on a jouncing tractor.

But I'm wrong.

Pauline calls me for supper.

We eat.

She leaves to visit a lonely neighbor lady. I'm in the front room' playing chess and losing. Just then I look out the big window.

There's that darn crow again, standing in the garden right where I don't dare shoot for fear I'll hit the neighbor's house or a car coming home from work. They really zip down that hill when you don't expect them.

I pry the door open carefully, gun in hand, one hinge squeaks slightly.

Sammy takes off cawing and chuckling as he wings-it to the maple-grove where Louie is perched.

I climb back on the tractor, still carrying the shooter. Maybe he'll come hunting for handouts. They like to follow my tiller blades to gather worms. Still, I can't figure out why these crows are sticking around so late. That's not common at all! This must be a special day.

Sure enough, here comes Sam. He flies right into the east end of the field, spikes an earth worm on his bill and eyes me with a cool orb. I turn the tractor loose, traveling a good ten miles an hour. I carefully lay the gun across the steering wheel. I have the feeling this is my evening, my night for a shootout at the "OK Corral," a strange premonition I'm Wyatt Earp.

I hold the shotgun in one paw, shove my arm straight ahead—jouncing nearer those feasting birds, Sam and his sidekick, Louie.

The crows show no alarm. Old Droz *never* shoots on the run; Sam knows that's a fact. He's maybe fifty years old, has wise brain cells

But, for once, that crow guesses wrong. The tractor's careening! I'm running fast on purpose. The crow doesn't figure anything's wrong.

I say to myself: don't be careful; just point his general direction; now, pull the trigger.

"Bar-r-r-oooM!" the shotgun speaks-and-streaks.

Nola! You must know how this story ends after all this build up. I didn't take special pains, just shoved the gun over the "S" wheel and let go—a one-armed, pointing, generally snap-shot just the way Buck Jones shot from the hip. Hey! Didn't I say I was once a ten year old cowboy.

What a surprise, dead on!
Poor old Sammy, son of a long, distinguished line of Scandian crows, just "keels-over-on-his-nose-bill" and lays his head on a clod.

I park the tractor and run to him. Would you believe, there's something noble, a sort of aura around that dying bird? He's making peace with his Creator. His eyes are closed. I pick him up, see his throat's torn by shot, feel the life ebb away.

I'm truly sorry I hit him. Wish I could bring him back. I never felt quite this way—with wild things at death's door—before.

I am struck with the sensation that this bird is important; he dreaded leaving family affairs undone. I ruined all his summer plans. Beyond that, I get the feeling he is most upset because a lesser being unfairly fooled him. There's some kind of wisdom in crows; they feel superior to humans. They proclaim this with every "ca-a-a-w" they emit. Yes, I have bested him unfairly!

Poor old Sam! My garden will never be the same. His pard', Louie, is watching. He comes back next day, hoping to get even any way he can. I get off another shot. Of course I miss. It's clear I'll never be a crack shot like my brother, the trapper.

Fact is, I never hit another interloper this entire season, but Sam's now strung up on a pole—a warning to all. Yes, passing crows often circle a dead comrade, venting dismal cries. I've watched it happen.

Nevertheless, they don't give death a long stint; one quick ceremony and it's over.

They'll be back; they continue to thrive.

Sammy's corpse has a *bad* summer; I hate to keep him impaled on that pole.

When harvest's done, I'll cut him down and provide a decent tomb. We'll put his name on a handmade cross just the way we buried pets when I was a kid. Perhaps, I'm entering second childhood. Truth is, that bird, dying in my hands, left me full of regret at his passage to the sod.

My day of departure is not many years away. The Purple Shield agent upped my burial insurance two days ago (right around the time of Sammy's death). I've had nightmares since he quoted coffin prices; maybe I equated that with that crow's demise.

So long Sam! Rest good.

Note: In a letter, Pauline wrote to Nola Waite the following. "Around 5:50 this morning there was the biggest, noisiest racket outside you ever heard. There was a cluster of crows up in the cherry tree nearby. They were looking down at the pole where Dwight put the crow he shot yesterday. It sounded all the world like a bona fide wake. They carried on for some time; then they took wing. Two birds visited our yard when we attended church the following Sunday; they fled the moment our truck turned into the drive. Well, Nola, this is a strange letter. It is late and I must hobble off to bed. I enjoyed your last letter so much. Just thought I'd share this snippet with you."

AN ODE FOR THE ROAD

Behold! I am old
Doin' work as I'm told:
I keep all my wants in tether;
Sometimes I shy, when winter's wry.
And nothing fits together
But cold, inclement weather.

And due to these intense concerns
I lighten each daily task:
As old Time churns, as night returns
I have no plan to ask—just bask.

Not counseled by giants,
My mind primes no schemes
For recalcitrant tyrants
Or rosy-nose queens—
Of pomp-and eclat.
I've cut my ambitions:
I'm proud of that.

Seek no land lords, no grand-boards,
Selling lots in a swamp!
No assessors,
Processors,
Or cheap-shots with pomp—
Shuck jailbirds and Yale-nerds;
End of tale; we must romp!

Note: Written in 1928.

A PICASSOAN LAMENT

There once was a painter, Picasso,
Whose work turned crass—like a simpering lass—
(Some"arty" morass-Progress-O!)
A bellicose roast, his motives toast—
For fanfare Rigoletto!

'Big-P' grew tired of antsy styles.
A rout! Due gout—or baddish bile.
His paintings changed; the mobs de-trained,
He grew morose the while.

Art nouveaus claim old Italy's main;
Pigtails, stuffed trams—migraine.
Rialto's ramps—lured luminous tramps
Toting easels up culture's drains.

Those blokes made jokes of Dutchies and Greeks,
Pests at-the-fests, those 'plastered' sheiks
Parked on a stump, to blithely paint
The patronage grumbles here were faint.

Old Gondoliers while patching leaks
Waved hungry hands to beggar tweaks.
At Bach or Beethovens these newcomers balk;
Then came the Beatles! Coca-Colanish-hawks,
Fat savants-in-berets, no shirt—and no socks:
'Two-Dog Nightly' sorts of flamboyant flocks!
And how they can rock!

Some ride on scooters for yin or fer yang;
In clutches; spray glutches of smoke—and go Bang!
With Fagan-like action while ruts fly beneath—
Like Heathcliff a-tiff at Thrushcross Heath.

Buying cheap paints, mid taints of some cachet;
They unroll a canvas and scratch ah-yet.
Some hit McDonald's (P.T.) for cash relief,
Painting wobbly strokes past all belief.
With wild bursts of color, the paint's all gone.
Piling layer on layer, they just pour on.

Be grumpy, gallumpy and crotch-a-tay!
Painting Picassian scenes in some frowsy way.
You could don an eye patch for underhand-clout;
Don't worry, most strangers won't figure it out.

If ya don't have a clue of what yer up to,
This is what artists expect of you.
Old timers may know your art is 'a-skewed';
But nowadays almost nobody is rude;
(What most men expect is pastels in the Nude!)
So don floppy-sandals be courteous, old dude—
Tell some guy with dough
He's the peak of your show.

When folks can't tell a bottom or top
Tell 'em you planned it for an easy swap.
Be busy-as-bizness'; *buy* easels—a booth;
Act easy-and-rich, though shorn in the tooth.
Be clutchy as teasel, you hearty, young weasel;
And—Don't fall apart!
Cause nobody here really understands art!

Epilog Amid the Smog
Most poets train without much strain;
Old artists have weak eyes.
What some folks link-to makes me blink.
Some buy things they despise; I surmise.
Some sling a brush, like stirring mush.
What prices, then, they post!

Causing bungling-dudes bad interludes—
Near-shocked as Hamlet's ghost!

Still, spending coins on 'art-annoyins'—
(Annoyances is partly the word.)
They haunt yard sales and bugger up tales
Of wonder-buys deferred. (Haven't you heard?)
Odd\old neckties—shoes with hooks for ties—
Stop! Ponder here a spell;
That face of Uncle—Sid,
By red-whiskers hid,
Might be the *best* to sell.
(I know it well.)

That's how the land lies;
Use expertise!
A show of pride, en-sasso:
And now, my dear, I exit here
With a "Yo! Ho!—Whoa!
Picasso."

ARATHENS AND ANTINENS

I woke up from repugnant sleep
Counting morays 'stead of sheep
Called arathens and antinens
Before slab-slates or fountain pens—
With a knot of schoolboy odds-and-ends
The title page wuz "It All Depends!"

Here forays start and stories end
With ampersands and twitty trends
If circles twist straight or ruler bends—
I still won't lie to you, my friends—
In came two monks with tails both ends;
    this isn't natural at all!
Then, Lewis Carrol came to call
That Maitre'D of *Ne'er-do-alls*—
Like gluts of smuts in old ink-stalls
That small boys spill on their overalls.

A chorus of lads with sobbing notes
Regaled me with discordant throats—
A vain respite of *sappy-songs*
Wearing blacksmith aprons seared by tongs
Like a Harry-Carey sing-along!

Now, I am a Hollander with bull boats whizzing by
Puff-cheek clouds, weary crowds
    piering from the sky
(A verbish word—and not a noun—
An Englishman here, I fear, would drown!)
Here arathens and antinens thrive thick as crabs,
Where farm boys never heard of cabs,
So-o-o, morays *mort*, and stories end—
    I'm only half-awake, old friend!

Wedged with antithen and antinens.
(No dictionary harbours them.)
So if ya have a *definish*,
Dear "Ed," please net some *micro-fiche*!
    Nuff sed.

Note: Harry Carey was a cowboy actor, best I remember, in the twenties. Nineteen hundreds, not the *two-thou'-plenties*. There were no computers or programmed liars. Just pen and ink—with bullfrog choirs. And patches all over Hen-Ford tires.

LITTLE PATHS

I'd rather follow a little path
    than trudge a grudging street
On a trickling, lazy lane of earth
    where dandelions meet.
You see a lone lark soaring high;
    you share the wind and sun!
Or walk, with errant footsteps, nigh—
    beneath an errant moon.

A byway may seem lonely
    'til a wild rose wins your heart;
For they let our tired souls forget
    a crowd—the joust—the mart.
O, there's not a friend on the broad world's side
    can share regrets or blues
Like dusty paths that wend away
    to the haunts of a wandering Muse:
For, it shares the lust of deserts, broad,
    that thirst for want of rain,
Or ambles down an aimless bank
    on some forgotten lane.

No need to bleat, or plod concrete,
    like lost lambs roam the fold;
To trail the mirth of "power and birth"
    on faces masked with gold.
O! I'd rather travel, a little way,
    on byways few men find;
For thoroughfares have lofty airs—
    but little paths are kind.

Note: Old Poem written for "The House By The Road," my Program over radio station KIDO, in Boise Hotel, circa 1938.

ONLY OF WOOD

"It is only of wood," the maestro said,
        and he shook his head and laughed,
As he fondled a bit of wood and glue
        that a child could break in half.
Yet, over the wood he bent his brow,
        as he drew the quivering bow,
And the violin spoke of beauties fled
        only a song could know.

What a fragile quill, the poet thought
        idly twirling a shaft
Of a feather smudged with ink and clot,
        the symbol of his craft;
Yet, to the sheet he plies with care,
        laboring with steadfast zeal,
As he dreams of the crown the scribe may wear
        for telling the truths we feel.

While idlers lie in the balmy sun,
        as the poor and the rich seek gold,
Old poets labor at tasks half-done,
        unmindful of warmth and cold:
And God, who made us of common clay,
        must judge his labor good
That summons us to dance and pray
        with a mere bit of glue and wood!

Note: One of my very earliest poems.

OTHER BOOKS BY DWIGHT R. DROZ
Available from Scandia Patch Press
http://kdkragen.com/scandia

One For The Weather, One For The Crow (with Pauline Droz)

Arizona Bound (with artwork by Annie Campbell)

Culture On The Cuff, V.1: Declo Days And Other Tall Tales

Culture On The Cuff, V.2: Cotterel, Heglar And Albion

Culture On The Cuff, V.3: Jack Simplot's Empire

Culture On The Cuff, V.4: The Marble Parrot And Other Tales

Printed in the United States
15723LVS00002B/1-63